DOWN *and* BACK

DOWN AND BACK

DOWN *and* BACK

A Guide to Living Happy with Depression

BY JULIA NOVAK

For reprint permission please contact the author at:
julia@julianovak.net
www.julianovak.net

ISBN 978-1-7323191-0-3 (paperback)

ISBN 978-1-7323191-1-0 (ebook)

Colophon
Interior Design by Renee Settle, 12 Minutes A Day LLC

Table of Contents

Dedication

To Phillip, Katia, and Zoe
You always believed

To Mama
Your love for books led me

Acknowledgements

I gratefully acknowledge my loving friends Yvonne Hayward, Lars Rasmussen, and Karen Cooper who held the vision of this book with me. And to Christina Rathbun, Georgie Robinson, Lisa Riddiough, Gina Vance and Celenia Delsol, thank you for your feedback and support as early readers.

And to my publishing consultant, Renee Settle. Thank you for your dedication, humor, and trust in divine timing.

Introduction

You know all about depression; what it looks, feels, and sounds like, all the causes and cures. And, you have probably tried all kinds of things to get out of it, deal with it, and get rid of it. You know all the reasons why you're depressed, and they are probably legitimate. You already know a lot. I get that.

What I'd like you to consider is that even though you know a lot, this might be the time in your life when you hear things differently. With an open mind, it's possible to understand something old in a new way. What if something has changed in you and you can now see yourself and your life in a way you never could before? Maybe recent events pushed you to the brink and made you desperate for answers. Maybe you've found peace and the willingness to let go of old ways to keep it. It took what it took to get you to this point. You've stumbled upon this book now for a reason. It's all about timing.

Timing is when events, people, and understanding come together just as they are supposed to when they are supposed to. It doesn't matter how much you've pushed to make something happen if it is not the right time, it ain't gonna happen. It's like forcing a baby to be born or a plant to grow. Some things require a natural (divine) schedule beyond our control. The conditions must be right for something new to take form. Looking back at my life, I see the timing in action and all the ways I missed it or used it to improve my health and happiness.

Despite seeking help early on to live with depression, I was slowly dying with it; getting further away from myself spiritually and emotionally, circling a desire for early physical death. Even with an emotional vocabulary and spiritual tools, I spent years trying to build a "normal" life with one hand as I fended off depression with the other. That's not living, that's battling.

For me, the timing as far as "succeeding" in life took far longer than I'd hoped. Ironically, I understand now that my desire to get rid of depression kept me from healing and opening to a more peaceful, fulfilling life. Now I am genuinely living with depression in the sense that I have an incredible landscape of emotions, beliefs, and experiences open to me that includes a place for depression.

Depression is not my entire world; it is part of it. A world that I consciously create through using ideas, and processes that I've accumulated and practiced, and now joyfully share with you. I'm not saying that you have to do exactly what I do or have done to stay alive and thrive. I offer the things that helped when I was hopelessly depressed and unable to break through, that reached the part of me who was so committed to being in pain and didn't know it. The me for whom "nothing worked."

I'm not a doctor and don't pretend to have all the answers, but I've been through enough life with depression caused by trauma, heredity, postpartum hormones, and the death of loved ones to have found some ways to move through it and live.

If you think things don't work for you, just maybe the timing is right, and there's something new here that might click. If you think you know it all, this is definitely for you. If you believe your history and genetics condemn you to a life of misery, please give these pages a chance and let it be a possibility for you.

By doing so, you'll find a new perspective on depression that turns your experiences in a more positive direction. You'll discover your innate power and the infinite wisdom of your Spirit that's been there all along.

You'll learn to listen to the needs of depression and heed the call to a happier life and understand how to build a bridge from despair and sadness to contentment and ultimately, to living your life purpose – to just be more of who you are.

Chapter 1

MY STORY

I left Kansas on a warm June morning in 1983 with cow shit stench wafting through the window from the feedlot five miles away. My parents stood in the driveway shoulder to shoulder, teary-eyed, waving goodbye. They figured I'd turn around before I made it to Uncle Joe's house in Denver. I had $300 in my wallet with my mom's new credit card for emergencies and a trunk filled with everything I owned. I had no job waiting and no real plan – other than crashing on the couch of a college buddy for a month while I looked for work.

It's a long flat freeway with nothing breaking the horizon for six hours from Great Bend to Denver. Acres of wheat turned green to gold, lush hay swirled and bent in the breeze, ready to be cut and bailed into huge rolls, and the occasional pumping unit slowly dipped its head toward the earth, as if lapping up the crude oil for the lucky family who owned the land. I spent an uneasy night in Uncle Joe's basement, helping myself to a few beers from the little frig behind his bar. In the morning Aunt Rusty made me pancakes, smoking menthol cigarettes as she sipped coffee and watched me eat.

Interstate 80 stretched across Wyoming like a long lonely ribbon through rolling hills and wide-open space, often without a living soul to be seen. I propped a novel on top of the steering wheel and read to pass the hours, glancing from book to windshield to make sure I was still in my lane.

The Wasatch Mountains rose in Utah like unwelcoming fangs pressing in on the narrow highway. I was a flatlander and had never driven in the mountains. Big rigs whizzed by me on the downhill, rattling my car and my nerves as I passed a screaming yellow sign announcing a Runaway Truck Ramp in 500 feet. I banked through curves and braked to stay under control, wondering if I could use the exit if I needed. My eyes darted to the rearview mirror, wary of things bigger than me sneaking up behind me.

A pink neon clown in downtown Reno beckoned me to stay the night, but I got screwed up by the one-way streets and missed the entrance to Circus-Circus hotel. A golden lion located down the block was my next choice, so I pulled into the new MGM Grand Casino, grateful to find liquid courage flowing freely from the bar after a dry night in uptight Salt Lake City. My courage didn't last when I awoke to a fire alarm clanging in the middle of the night. I called my mom despite the hour, unsure if I should leave my room or wait out the noise.

In a few days, I'd traded dirt roads for 8-lane freeways. A high narrow bridge, my first of many in the Bay Area, carried me across what looked like a lake. Far below gray battleships anchored at an empty shore, ghostly and out of place.

Once off the freeway, I snaked past taquerias and low riders, small working-class cottages with palm trees and bright flowers, and tiny Vietnamese women crouched at a bus stop. Strange faces I'd never seen in my white bread world were everywhere, speaking tongues I couldn't understand. As I drove the last block to my friend's apartment complex, the sharp scent of eucalyptus poured through the open window, clearing my nose but nothing else..

My head spun when my feet finally touched down in California, blown by the storm of my life in Kansas. I thought it would be better than where I'd been. I was wrong. This was just the start of my real search for home.

I'd grown up outside a small town in a big, ranch style house made of dark red brick that sat at the end of a sweeping driveway. There were wide open pastures to the north and east and nothing to slow the wind or block the sky.

From the outside, our lives looked like we were well-off, but we weren't. My parents built our house when I was six by working hard and doing much of the labor themselves. Mom took in sewing and cared for foster kids besides her own six children to help make the mortgage payment. Dad quit his job to work as an electrical contractor in 1973 and grew a thriving business he and my brothers still run to this day. We were well fed on a clockwork schedule, wore stylish homemade clothes, and always had enough to open at Christmas. I had siblings and dogs and a wide-open space around me to play in, but I was never happy.

Before the big red brick house, we'd lived in a little white house on Washington Street. Without a bedroom of my own, I slept on one half of the couch in the living room with my little brother. If I slept, that is. I was a roamer, sleepless and wandering with my homemade pink blanket in hand. Sometimes I crawled into the old baby crib in mom and dad's room or curled up at the foot of their bed in the bedspread that fell halfway to the floor. If I was brave enough to ask, and then lucky, they let me in bed next to them when I whispered their names.

Night time was scary. That's when I heard and saw and felt everything. So, I played with the toys in the big drawer in the bathroom or looped around the living room talking to my imaginary cat. On hot summer nights, I stopped at the window air conditioner, put my "blankey" in front of the vents, then walked in a circle and picked it up – sticking my thumb in my mouth while I pulled the cool soft cotton across my top lip and under my nose.

It was in this little house, my life took a wrong turn. My 14-year-old sister Terri accidentally smothered me to death on the living room floor. I was three years old. No one knew but her because I died and came back again before anyone else noticed. I grew up with no memory of that day, but my guess now is that she got annoyed with my little kid noise and wanted me to shut up. Maybe she needed me quiet because she couldn't quiet her rage and fear bubbling up in her life.

If she realized what happened and remembered it, Terri never told me, even as she slowly weakened then died just after her 56th birthday. She'd refused chemotherapy after her breast cancer returned and wound up suffocating as tumors slowly filled her lungs. At the time I felt she was punishing herself for giving up, doing penance for some deed the rest of us didn't understand. The night before she died, she called from Kansas. I'd just returned home with my daughters Katia and Zoe, then 10 and 6, after spending two weeks with her. The plan was to get them settled and go back to Kansas a week later to help take care of Terri. My husband Phillip answered the phone and listened quietly as she thanked him over and over for helping me visit her and keep her well.

When I took the phone, she spoke in a whisper, repeatedly murmuring "I'm sorry, I'm sorry," and finally saying "I love you," before hanging up. I thought she was apologizing for leaving us too soon but feel now if it was something more. I never saw her again.

Not long after Terri died, I started having flashbacks of dying. Grief and depression forced me back into therapy, and each time I came near the source of my pain in a session, my mind would go blank. Sometimes I would fall asleep in the therapist's chair and appear unconscious. But each time my mind let me see more. Slowly, images and feelings returned. I was small, on my back, kicking and punching at someone above me smashing my face and throat with their hands. My chest crumpled and burned as the air left me. Then, nothing. Although I re-experienced this memory for a long time, I wasn't sure who I was fighting. Years later with guidance and more insight, I came to understand, and it explained why for much of my life I vaguely sensed I shouldn't be here, unconsciously aligning my life to make that false belief come true. I never felt angry at Terri because I know she loved me and never meant to hurt me.

My sister's rage didn't come out of nowhere. She was a victim too, of a family friend who molested me when I was five years old and abused her as a young teenager. She often babysat for his daughters, who were about the same age as our other sister and me. We played at their house and had sleepovers with his girls.

I have a memory of standing in a closet hiding behind heavy clothes covering my face and robbing me of air. I feel doomed. I can't save myself. There is no one there to help me. That fear etched itself into my bones. It moved with me, taking a different shape as I grew.

I learned there are two ways to get out of the dark – turn on a light or deny that you're afraid. My path took me into drowning my fear. I was five years old the first time I got drunk after polishing off a half bottle of cheap pink wine I took from the refrigerator. I drank every chance I got – refilling my grandpa's juice glass with Mogen David wine for him, but only after I knocked back a glassful. Or stealing cups of beer off of trays carried around family weddings dances, pretending to get it for my parents, then drinking until I passed out. I was six.

At 10, I stashed vitamins, aspirin, and Midol in a fake leather purse hanging in my closet – all part of my naïve plan to run away to the creek and kill myself.

For months, I'd plotted and collected those pills, confident I'd feel better once I was dead. I wondered about how long it would take before anyone realized I was gone and if they would miss me. I didn't know then that what I wanted was for someone to notice I was already gone – in a dark place with no light and no words for it. But depression in children wasn't talked about in those days, and certainly not in my family. Words like ungrateful, moody, stubborn, and morose were used instead. My mother's standard line was "You're never happy," though she tried to make me that way. Eventually, the pills were discovered and tossed away, and my opportunity with it.

I don't remember what pushed me over the edge to that decision to die when I was 10, but I remember the feeling and the voice in my head because it's been with me ever since. When I reach back in time, the weight and blackness of depression sit at the bottom of my heart, squeezing the breath from my lungs, souring my stomach, and tighten my pelvis with fear and suspicion.

It's said depression is a manifestation of repressed anger. Perhaps anger is also what drove me at school, to get straight A's, win speech contests and spelling bees; to become the newspaper editor, pep club president, a cheerleader, and a self-proclaimed bitch. But that voice insisted my accomplishments weren't enough, and it quickly pointed out my failures, so nothing I did ever felt like a success.

By the time I attended college at the University of Kansas in 1979, I was drinking three times a week. I'd looked good on the outside back home in my small town with good grades, a cute boyfriend, a big house. I'd blustered my way through high school, confident I knew how to do things right and get what I wanted. That ability dissipated within weeks at the university where I felt like a little fish in a big pond with no idea how to compete, belong, and thrive. By the end of college, I drank to oblivion four days a week and lived alone, rooted in depression.

The grace of intuition put me on the road to California two weeks after graduation. It should have been exciting. It should have been fun. I told myself, "My life is starting now, and things will be different."

But Depression drove with me across the country, sitting in the front seat next to Extreme Fear.

The heaviness of depression took me back to the bottle over and over, clouding my judgment and killing my ambition. I'd come to California hoping to work in public relations, but jobs were scarce. I eventually wound up in a sales job with a bunch of older men who liked to drink at lunch and go to happy hour at the bar around the corner after work. I fit right in and could hold my own with the booze. Over the next year, daily drinking became part of my routine to cover my fear and anxiety about work and a failing relationship. My drinking problem was becoming harder to deny.

I "woke up" after hitting bottom at 25, my body sick from the constant overdose of sugar in the booze, paralyzed with fear and depression, and unable to make myself get up and go to work. I checked into a rehab hospital and, although I never drank again, I spent years pulling myself out the same dark hole.

I'd opened to facing down my demons, and along the way found that I had a direct connection to the light I'd been holding back as well. I discovered my intuitive gifts and sensitivities as I changed paths to a spiritual road, free of the judgmental God I learned about in Catholic school. But even my spiritual awakening didn't save me as I bumped up against my past, postpartum depression, and what I still believed was my real, broken nature.

Saving myself in sobriety took me deep into self-reflection and the need for understanding, not only about my physical and emotional life but my spiritual life. I nervously sat for my first psychic reading in 1986 where I was promptly told I should do what she was doing. After moving the next year to Wisconsin, I took my first meditation class with a woman who developed spontaneous psychic ability after her own near-death experience. I studied divination tools, spent hours working with tarot cards, automatic writing, and numerology. I began masters' coursework in psychology and counseling at the University of Wisconsin but got interrupted by a move back to California.

In 1993, I became a licensed spiritual counselor after nearly two years of intensive training in Berkeley CA centered on developing my abilities as a clairvoyant. I spent hundreds of hours reading hundreds of people, learning to connect to others' Spirit, see and interpret their energy field, and stay neutral while doing it. I learned to meditate, and "manage" my energy field so I would not be at the mercy of other's emotions and energetic baggage. It's the emotional equivalent of doing ten years of psychotherapy in a year. It was intense, demanding and rewarding beyond belief as I tapped into truths I suspected buried deep inside of me.

In 1997, I began post-graduate work in Consciousness Studies at John F. Kennedy University. Being a full-time mom, a part-time psychic, and a freelance writer for local San Francisco Bay Area publications gave me access to spiritual leaders like channel Kevin Ryerson, and authors Starhawk and Anne Lamott. Attending many conventions and seminars on the growing spiritual and consciousness movement in those years exposed me to the work of leading-edge thinkers. I joined the Institute of Noetic Sciences and led a local chapter of the Intuition Network, dedicated to connecting others to the power of their intuition.

My ability to read people and intuitively know what's working and what's not in their energy field, and their life, continued to grow over the years. Early on I expanded my work to include diagnosing and healing the energy of places by doing what I call "intuitive feng shui" after training with disciples of Grandmaster Thomas Lin Yun, who brought the art of Black Sect Esoteric Buddhist feng shui to the United States.

I've returned to learning often over the years, with post-graduate coursework at UC Berkeley, and a year-long program focusing on the specific energetic issues of being in a female body.

In 2014, after the tragic death of my young daughter's friend, my mediumship ability opened up more to connect with the spirits of those who have passed away. I've been called to deepen that work, and those who seek me out for counseling often do so because of loss. My connection to those who have died allows me to communicate messages left unsaid, and to bring meaning to the relationships clients had with their loved ones this lifetime. Often, the purpose of their death – especially with tragic or early deaths – is clear when I communicate with them in a reading. I'm shown the context of the events of their life in the overall purpose they chose as a Spirit, and the lesson they came to work out in the time allowed.

As a counselor and psychic consultant, I help others see themselves as I see them – magnificent Spirits with lives created by them to learn. My goal is to bring Spirit down to Earth by inspiring them to open up and experience for themselves the Divine consciousness that flows through all things. I'm committed to sharing and relaying information in a way that people can understand and translate into tangible, practical action that shifts the quality and direction of people's lives toward the positive. After every session – whether a onetime reading or a series of meetings to address long-term changes, I give homework – useful and manageable information that can impact your life in the long run.

I've worked hard over the years to educate others about psychic ability and energy work to remove the stereotypes associated with it – crystal balls, taking money to remove curses – and the fear it brings up around religious and personal beliefs. I look and sound "normal" – a wife, a mom, a woman with problems like everyone else – so the stereotype changes from something fearful into something safe and even inspiring. Others can see their capacity for having a "superpower" and a direct connection to something infinitely bigger and wiser than they believed possible.

What I know now is that everyone has a story. Some stories are worse than others. I used to think my story wasn't sad enough to justify feeling depressed, so I had no excuse for failing to get the things I wanted and live a happy, productive life. My idols and mentors had it much worse growing up, yet they made something of themselves. Why couldn't I?

On the other hand, I felt so broken and powerless. No way could I have a happy life. I compared myself to those people and thought I wasn't as smart or resilient. Things weren't bad enough, I wasn't good enough. I never let myself win.

Every story on the road to Depression is important. You don't have to be majorly screwed up to achieve great "success," nor does a screwed up past mean you have to stay stuck. The important thing is not to get caught in one or both beliefs because then you are screwed. That was me – but not anymore.

Chapter 2

CREDIT FOR THE SMALL THINGS

My client Nina shoots awake every morning with a racing heart and a stab of fear in her gut, followed by dread as she recites the previous day's failures. She tells me, "I didn't make that call I promised I'd make. I didn't go to yoga again. Damn, I forgot to get a birthday card for mom."

She should spend the day making jewelry for a craft fair to help launch her new business, but the idea exhausts her before she even raises her head from the pillow. Worry floods her mind, speaking loud and clear. *Will my daughter make it to school today or will she have another panic attack and stay in bed? Will my son's grades be good enough to get him into college? Did he even finish the applications as he said? If he gets in, we can't pay for it if I don't make money. I have to get my business off the ground. Time is running out. I can't keep wasting it.*

It's enough to make anyone breathless with fear.

Nina wants to be like her friend Jennifer who breezes through life. She's a local girl and knows everyone. She married her college sweetheart and had two cute kids who kick ass on the soccer field and swim team. Her hubby makes good money and loves to do remodeling

13

projects for fun, so there's never a "honey-do list" argu-
ment between them. Their house looks like it's straight
out of a home décor magazine. She has a family vacation
home at the lake where she spent summers growing up,
and now her kids do the same. Jennifer works part-time,
volunteers at the school. She belongs to book, bunco, and
bocce clubs and has family nearby to help her whenever
she needs it. She likes to entertain and acts casual and
relaxed with a house full of people. Her life is good. This
town is her place, her community and she belongs here.
She's a success in every way.

When we meet, Nina asks, "Why can't I do what I
want to do with my life? Why can't I be who I want to
be?" The questions swirl around her all day long, numbing
her with paralysis.

Nothing gets done, nothing changes. Nina feels like a
loser, living the same life, year after year, despite knowing
what she wants. Depression has taken over and embodied her. She drifts, speaks quietly, and has no energy or
enthusiasm for anything in her life.

To Nina, a happy life lies "someday" out in the future.
When she finally meets expectations and accomplishes
her goals, then she'll be a "success." After all, isn't it the
success that brings happiness? But no matter what she
does or has done, it's never enough.

***

We live in a constant state of not-enough-ness. What
we have, what we do, who we are falls short of the image
of a happy, successful life. This critical self-judgment is a
bright thread running through the tapestry of our life we
use to measure our ability and experience against others.

Now, social media wildly increases the opportunities
to judge ourselves and makes feeling "not enough" an

overwhelming force influencing our emotional well-being. This is especially true for younger generations tied to their phones. We suffer a daily barrage from social media and television saying, "look at what I have, who I know, what I did." It only takes 10 minutes of looking at Facebook to have a vague sense something is wrong with us. The fear of missing out, falling behind, and being irrelevant creeps up on the best of us, eroding our sense of self.

Depression feeds on this attention by showing us what is lacking in ourselves. The more we see what's missing from our lives, the more it feels true when we tell ourselves we are worthless. With mounting evidence of what we can't do, or don't have, depression easily keeps us from pursuing dreams and goals, proving again that things just don't work for us.

Like Nina, I suffered from that feeling of "not enough-ness" and created unrealistic expectations about how a good life should look. Being happy meant being successful. Being successful meant being happy.

Often happiness, which for me really meant the absence of depression, existed somewhere in the future. I often thought to myself, "When I publish my first book, I'll feel complete. When the kids are older and don't require so much attention, I'll pursue my dreams. When I lose weight, I'll be happy."

This future-driven perspective is like looking at a mountain peak off in the distance with blinders on – all the lofty hopes are beautiful to look at – but we miss everything at our feet. We don't enjoy the meadow full of wildflowers, the light, and shadow playing against the trees, or the animals grazing nearby. We miss the steps carved in the path that takes us to the top, and the others along the way who can help us. Looking through a limited lens of "someday" obscures how far we've come.

That feeling of "not-enough-ness" kept me from succeeding for years. I'd gather enthusiasm to tackle my plans and dreams for a month, then get sucked back into despair, believing things will never work or I can't do it because things didn't turn out the way I thought they would. I'd give up at the first sign of failure or chase off after another project or guru, convinced that what I'd been doing wasn't the right path since it didn't work immediately. I'd isolate, get bogged down in the routine of daily housework and children and settle into motherhood mindlessly. Convinced I'm only capable of managing housework and errands I'd recommit to a life devoted to my daughters' care, all the while feeling pulled toward a need to do my creative work, make my own money, and give to the world in some way while still being a good mom and partner.

When I didn't meet the standards I'd set for myself, I had no problem finding reasons to live in depression. It was easy to define myself by my past as a victim or an alcoholic and convince myself I deserved to despair. But, by looking at my life through the veil of depression, I couldn't see what I have as a foundation to build on.

What kept me stuck was having an unrealistic definition of success and how to achieve it, and the inability to give myself credit for anything. No matter what I'd done or how hard I worked, I never celebrated a win. I could always find fault in my effort or discount my actions as not important enough – everyone does it, not a big deal.

Success recognizes any action I take that validates the life I want, speaks to who I am and lifts me, even for a split second, from despair into feeling connection is important.

Success is not the big accomplishments. It's all the little events that add up to create the life you want in a big way.

With the light of this new truth, I could see all the ways I succeed on a daily basis. It's this illumination I want to share with you in these pages. It's possible to define your success with or without depression at your side. It's how you define success that keeps you from it and feeds "not enough-ness." I offer some new possibilities.

For those of us prone to negativity, often mired in hopelessness, trauma, and sadness, success is choosing to look at any moment from a state of self-appreciation and self-love that aligns our wisdom, heart, and courage. From here, a meaningful life based on what's important to us and not on how we compare to others is possible. By living a life that feels meaningful and tied to the core of who we are, we then naturally move into an expansive, more fulfilling place.

It has nothing to do with money or material things although those things seem to come more easily when you live a meaningful life. What matters is the wealth of connection – to self, to others, to nature – to a sense of something infinite which is really the bigger ME that's been there all along, WHOLE, waiting for my unconscious self to wake up and reunite with it.

Success is noticing all the little ways I have been the whole me in my daily life: I was a good listener for my daughters. I reached out to a friend and had a great conversation. I fed myself healthy food. I went for a walk instead of watching TV; I took a nap when I grew tired instead of drinking coffee, I didn't criticize my husband's driving. I admitted I didn't know something, asked for help and felt ok about it instead of feeling stupid. I gave up being angry at my family and told them what I felt instead of going silent for days expecting them to apologize and change.

Success for me now is catching myself thinking negatively, stopping mid-thought and saying "no, that's not true," or "no, I don't want to feel bad about this. I get to choose." It's when I remember I can control my thoughts; my thoughts don't control me. It's when I deeply understand that all the crap that happened in the past is in the past and has absolutely nothing to do with today. Today I can be anyone I want to be emotionally. Today I can have any thought I want to have. They are all new and NOW.

Success is anytime I can think, feel, and act from a lighter place and welcome that into my life-like noticing the sound of the wind high in the trees or the vivid pink of a flower out my window. It's looking up to the birds and clouds overhead instead of having tunnel vision as I hurry along from place to place. It is looking in my daughters' eyes when they speak rather than staring at a screen or busily multi-tasking.

Success is dropping my awareness into my body and noticing the tension or pain there, breathing through it, and asking "what do I need?" and then feeling better at the moment when I get an answer.

Success is cultivating a quietly extraordinary life starting from inside myself through reflection, a beautiful inner landscape where I meet my true self. And the more I visit and honor that inner beauty the more it shows up in "real" life externally as new friends, better health, a good marriage, happy children, and renewed creativity.

Redefining success opened me up. Before I knew it, I did the things I always said I wanted to do but never could-like spending hours in my studio writing short stories, articles and a novel, filling my consulting practice with new clients, honoring my skills, and living my beliefs.

I feel connected to myself, my home, my community, my family, and the world – and I can help others feel that way too.

All the small successes add up and then, life shifts. I was a week or a month or even a year down the road when I realized I haven't felt depressed. I recognized when my emotions were heading downhill and stopped, changed course, and moved back to brighter moments. Not by running away from it, but by calling out its name. We redefine success by taking credit for any action that lifts us out of the negative view of "not enough" and points us in a fortunate direction. We're no longer a failure, but a success every day, in some way.

Chapter 3

YOU'RE NOT CRAZY, YOU'RE JUST PSYCHIC

Olivia secretly feared she was a hypochondriac. For years she suffered from physical pain and unexplained ailments, but doctors found nothing wrong with her when she sought medical help. Symptoms came and went, for no reason. Nothing made sense. Depression and anxiety plagued her as she doubted herself and her sanity. Some days, she thought she was crazy. It took years to figure out that she's not a hypochondriac, but rather a highly sensitive empath and psychic, especially when it came to her family. She often experiences her loved ones' illness pre-cognitively in her own body, without knowing who will be in distress.

On a recent evening, she felt agitated and restless. She became nauseous and then developed pain in her low abdomen. As the night wore on, she could not sleep, and her pain increased. Because she trusts that not everything she experiences is her own, she tried to stay alert and "listen" to her body and her feelings. Olivia also knows now that the experiences that keep her up all night usually have to do with a soul leaving the body or deciding to go or stay.

That night, she felt the presence of her deceased father's spirit, and could sense him telling her "I've got it, it's okay." Exhausted, she finally fell asleep at 4 am, only to receive a call from her nephew later that morning. His wife, who is close to Olivia, miscarried their twins during the night. Olivia felt the devastation but knew that the twins were in good hands with her father.

***

For me, getting sober woke me up to the fact I am a highly sensitive person. And like me, many of my clients are highly intuitive, empathic, and often psychic and suffer from cyclical bouts of depression, or at least a low-grade dullness, disconnection, and disinterest in life.

Being intuitive is a universal ability revealed in our daily language: "It came to me off the top of my head," "I had a gut feeling," "Something told me..." "I saw it coming."

These experiences occasionally happen to everyone, but some of us have them more than most and don't realize it, or pick up even more information beyond the scope of the five senses.

Depression is a response to an unrecognized psychic and intuitive ability that is out of control. It is a spiritual 'affliction' and something that is brought on or exacerbated by, biological and neurological mechanisms. What if you're not crazy, you're just psychic?

What do I mean by intuitive and psychic? In simple terms, you can say that someone who is psychic is highly intuitive. Intuition is knowing, without knowing how you know – it's direct access to information or truth without reasoning it through.

Psychic abilities are extra-sensory perceptions that lie outside the realm of physical or scientific knowledge or reasoning, like telepathy or clairvoyance (clear seeing) or clairaudience (clear hearing) or clairsentience (clear feeling).

When you're empathic, you automatically pick up on the feelings or "vibes" of people, places or even things. Empaths are sensitive and easily hurt. They are usually introverted and require alone time to reset and feel like themselves. Empathic and psychic ability, when you're aware of it, is a wonderful gift – a "superpower" that opens you to ideas, inspiration, and clarity that can propel you through life. When you're not aware, it's a curse that creates a roller coaster of emotions and experiences too hard to handle. Life seems like too much.

Being empathic is like being a fish in water. If you could speak to the fish and ask, "what's it like to be in the water?" it would reply, "what's water?" If you're accustomed to the energy surrounding you in a particular way, you do not know what it is your swimming in – it's your normal.

When you're empathic, you feel and experience everything around you as your own. Just like the water around the fish, every movement within it creates a ripple, large or infinitesimal, that reverberates around the whole environment. Whether a puddle, a lake, or an ocean, it's a closed system of experience. Picking up on those movements is a matter of degree of awareness, raising the question: Is this coming from me or at me?

The same applies to our unique energy field, or aura, that connects to the global ocean of energy surrounding us all; the Earth's electromagnetic field. We live in a closed energetic system of frequency and color, just like the one system of air and water that circulates our planet. We're breathing the same air the dinosaurs breathed. The water we drink today was once rainfall in the Himalayas or a glacier in the Arctic.

Technical instruments distinguish the difference between x-rays and gamma rays, between blue and red on the energy spectrum, but the sensitive machine that we are doesn't always accurately register and define what we pick up. Like that fish, it is hard to distinguish where we begin and end because it is our "normal."

This ability to discern includes emotional and physical experiences. Without understanding your energy field and separation from others, you will assume your feelings are yours. But what if much of the sadness, anger, frustration, fear that you feel daily has nothing to do with you? What if you are merely a magnet for energy and emotions, a dumping ground sometimes, for other people's stuff? What if you are a supremely capable "noticer" and your awareness is so high that you are seeing, smelling, hearing, and feeling things that most people miss entirely? What if you're not crazy, or lazy, or wrong, you're psychic?

Because it is normal for you, you assume most people experience and process life the same way. There's no conversation about it to compare notes. Most likely, you can't even name what you experience because it is so unconscious.

But why is it you get exhausted by crowds or attract friends and family or even strangers with nothing but problems? Why are you afraid for no reason, or sick all the time with unexplained or chronic illness? Why do loud noises or strong smells overwhelm you? Why do you feel like crying or have an unexplainable aversion to certain places or people? Why don't you sleep well? Why are you heartbroken as you pass a swath of cut down trees, or mounds of earth dug up for yet another subdivision?

Because you're overloaded. You don't know how to discern what is your life force energy and experience, and what is a reaction to someone else's – including nature and Earth itself. As a result, it's difficult to connect to and create your own life.

Now imagine the fish inside a bubble while floating seamlessly through the ocean of its life. This bubble allows the fish to see, interact, and move. To engage and let others in its "space" as it sees fit. The fish senses changes in its immediate environment within that sphere and can decide how to act, think and feel without being overly influenced by outside forces. This is the path to take as an empath. We need our bubble, and the first step is awareness.

Consider your life from the perspective of being an energetic or psychic sponge. Who and what surrounds you? What are the thoughts, beliefs, words, music, sounds, and smells filling your inner and outer world? What do you look at all day? What are you choosing to steep yourself in energetically?

Do you believe, "I live this way because I'm depressed," when it could be you're depressed because of how you live?

As a sensitive person, it's essential to create your own "bubble" by being the dominant energy in your life. I'll discuss later how you can set the tone – the vibration of your life – and manage the amount and kind of energetic input you receive.

In hundreds of sessions over 25 years, I've seen people unaware of this shared ability to feel, know, see and hear beyond the usual five senses that influence them on a powerful emotional level. I see the effects of empathic sensitivity in the amount and types of energy that they hold in their body and auric field. I hear it in the stories they tell of being in emotional and physical pain often time with no direct logical connection to anything that's happening in their life.

They anxiously talk of not knowing how to change, or how to make decisions. I hear it too when they express fear of knowing too much because they sense coming events, and when they happen, it's frightening. They misunderstand their precognition and believe they are causing things to happen. If what they see coming isn't positive, it shuts them down to knowing anything; suppressing the good with the bad.

Research psychology documents these empathic and intuitive traits from other helpful perspectives. Dr. Elain Aron in *The Highly Sensitive Person*[1] defines one trait of a sensitive person as being aware of "subtleties of the environment," which I extend to energetic, empathic abilities. In *The Introvert Advantage*[2] author, Marti Olson Laney points out that our society supports an extroverted personality, but one out of three people are introverted (and by my definition, highly intuitive as well) and are trying to fit into a mold that doesn't suit them.

There are plenty of extroverted people who suffer from depression too. There are times when being in the world is too much for anyone and requires pulling back. It all comes down to balance. I fall in the middle as equally introverted as I am extroverted. I love to meet people, talk and get away from home to new places. I need change to stay inspired. But, I also can't take crowds or chaos. I require solitude, quiet, and focused creative time or I become a raging mess.

Recognizing yourself in traits shared by others can be a relief. Being different is not wrong, it is normal for you. The point is not to find a new "label" to identify with or to blame as the source of depression, but rather to look at yourself from a place of non-judgment and find out where your power lies. Sensitivity is a strength that requires care and attention to use it to its full potential.

The crush of sensitivity, once you recognize and understand it, shifts from being a curse of heavy emotions and overwhelm, to a gift of inner guidance and connection to self and others. Being intuitive and sensitive is a blessing for nurturers, artists, counselors, and visionaries. It's the gift of a new perspective that moves culture forward.

At a recent gathering, I spoke to Lauren about her onset of depression. Her eyes lit up when I told her sadness, and lack of energy could be an unrecognized psychic ability gone awry. As I described how being unaware of empathy puts us at the whim of everyone and everything around us, her eyes filled with tears.

"That's me. I see it now. I quit my job last week after 13 years. I couldn't do it anymore. I sat across from an angry woman who yelled hateful words into the phone all day. I thought it was just something wrong with me because I felt so bad all the time."

Relief flooded her face and body as she realized there might be another answer why she'd been so unhappy. Lauren said she'd been struggling all day to decide if she should take anti-depressants again after having been off of them for a year. She felt our conversation was perfect timing. It was an answer that felt true deep inside her.

I saw the wheels turn in her head as she thought about all the other ways she energetically took on other people's emotions and problems by being an over-responsible caretaker. I felt her exhaustion of being a people pleaser, a perfectionist, and a hard worker who rarely has fun. Suddenly she saw herself in a new way. She wasn't broken, she just misunderstood her wholeness.

Once you acknowledge that you're "not crazy" and at the mercy of life, or failing because you're not like others, you can focus on finding what works for you in a busy, energetic, chaotic world without giving up who you are. Remember that joy is as much your right as pain. There are ways to open up to and manage this sensitivity to work for you to live a happier life.

It requires looking at yourself with new respect by doing routine things to maintain your health on all levels. Appreciate that you are a "finely tuned instrument" that demands a certain environment to work or play as beautifully as intended. You require special care.

With great power comes great responsibility, and that's true of being psychically and empathically sensitive. Acknowledging your sensitivity opens the door to the positive potential you may never have considered. Stepping through the door demands that you accept the responsibility of taking care of yourself and therefore taking care of your gift.

We can't do it overnight. Recognizing, accepting, and taking responsibility is a process, a practice, and it grows stronger as we learn to give ourselves credit for the small things.

Like my highly empathic friend Olivia mentioned above. As she noticed how often she was "right" about her gut reactions, and paid attention to how her body was mirroring the world around her, she felt more in charge of herself and her life. One last episode convinced her of the immensity of her ability and pushed her to understand the blessing in her "curse."

Last summer, Olivia woke with a horrible stiffness and pain in her neck and shoulders, assuming it was caused by the yard work she did the day before. It persisted, making it difficult to lift her arms, so she got a massage and did other home remedies to help herself. Throughout July and August, the pain was barely under control. She "checked in" with herself and felt she didn't need to seek medical advice and assumed it was due to the stress of her only son leaving for college.

By September she realized it was something "energetic," and trusted her gut to get acupuncture treatments. The pain went away almost immediately.

Soon after she had lunch with an elderly aunt, who recounted her recent struggle when rheumatic myalgia erupted in her neck and shoulders in July. The pain was excruciating, and she could not lift her arms until finally in early September massive doses of drugs were administered, and her pain went away. It was obvious as she talked that the timing and intensity of her experience were the same as Olivia's.

Olivia left that lunch date stunned again by the intensity of her empathic ability. But more powerfully, she understood how important it was to find the way to heal herself in future instances. She realized that since she has these strong connections with others, it might be possible for it to go the other direction. So, the sooner she can heal, the sooner others will heal. And also, she believes now that by proactively staying healthy, she contributes to the health of those she loves. She sees the bigger purpose of understanding suffering is to help heal the world by radiating health and happiness – to send it back up her empathic line of connection to the collective consciousness that surrounds us all. It is her contribution and a powerful choice in taking what was so long a curse and making it work for good.

And though it may sound crazy, the best place to find the light of your wisdom is in the dark.

Chapter 4

DARKNESS

All things grow first in the dark. Seeds in the ground, a baby in the womb, a butterfly wrapped in a chrysalis. The darkness of depression is the place where new things can begin too. In the retracted, quiet place where depression lives there is an opportunity to grow.

Sometimes the only place you can truly see yourself is in the dark. Pulled away from life and in your underworld, the chance arises to adapt night vision that lets you see the roots of what is taking hold there.

In your underworld, no one can care for you, nor do you have anyone to care for. It is a place to meet your essence and learn. A place that can strengthen you. Dark times require that for at least some moment, you have to go it alone, do it alone, and be alone because no one else can change you. Darkness isn't always a bad thing.

Darkness in life is inevitable. We experience troubles and challenges no matter who we are. Being in the thick of it can bring us to a "dark night of the soul," a difficult place where questions about life's meaning and purpose, and loss of hope loom. These dark nights can come and go suddenly at the whim of outside circumstances or arrive as a soulful sadness and longing that drags on for months or years. But there is hope.

Thomas Moore, a spiritual writer and psychologist, champions the dark night as a source of growth and understanding.

"A dark night of the soul need not be depressing. Today we tend to think of all emotional negativity as depression, and so we imagine ourselves sometimes to be depressed when in fact it is only the world that is pressing down on us. You can be bright, thoughtful, creative, and imaginative during a dark night. You can use all your power to imagine your situation in your own way."[1]

The power to imagine lies in your sensitivity. What you tell yourself when you're in the dark has everything to do with how you feel. If like me, you are accustomed to feeling victimized by blaming others for your problems and giving up your power, then you will feel "bad" with no hope of relief. Life is an onslaught of problems.

Consider instead that when the world continues to press down on us with poor health and misfortune, we're being called by our Spirit to take notice. Darkness isn't meant to show us how we're broken, but rather how we're ready to grow.

Re-framing what you think about the darkness fueling depression using imagination and more gives you fresh eyes to see yourself and your life experiences. What if you let yourself sit in the darkness with an attitude of respect or curiosity and ask what is pushing you toward the light, like a seed sprouting underground? Welcome it as a sign of deep knowing seeking your attention, rather than a sign of defeat.

It's in refusing to heed the wisdom dark offers us that we stall out, pushing deeper into pain until we are forced to respond.

We're afraid sometimes to sit with our darkness because it feels destructive and may take us where we don't really want to go. That's why it's impossible to talk about depression without talking about death. To someone who's never experienced depression, wanting to die makes no sense, but, to us, it can. At the worst times when there seems no way out of pain, it circles our thoughts, sounding like a good option. But no matter what the circumstances, it is not. No one will be better off without you. If you feel that way now, stop reading and talk to someone immediately so you can move to a place of understanding, not ending. You can call the National Suicide Prevention Lifeline 24 hours a day at 1-800-273-8255.

Not everyone suffering from sadness and depression gets entranced by suicidal thoughts. Perhaps the dark holds an unspoken fear of death, either your own or another's, or you are suffering the loss of someone you love and can't yet grasp the finality. At times like these, we do need to reach out to find someone or something to light the way out of deep fear and grief. To find ways to deal with the inevitable. We are woefully unprepared for death in our modern culture. There are no myths or stories to help us understand and incorporate it as we grow up. Gone are the days when we observed or helped care for others as they died at home and held funerals and wakes in the living room. Death is a big business, sanitized and removed from our sight. No wonder we are afraid.

What if depression is a death of its own? What if it's a necessary place to draw from to be reborn or live in a new way? It calls for a different kind of death, not of the physical body, but of beliefs, pain, and the past. Like the Death card in Tarot which symbolizes rebirth as much as death, teaching us that accepting death doesn't require leaving our body behind.

I often turn to the archetypal imagery of Tarot cards to widen and deepen my perspective to understand my emotional challenges. Archetypes are recurrent symbols or motifs that appear universally in art, literature, and mythology and connect us to primal images found in the collective unconscious.

The Death card reflects the principle of letting go and moving forward through transition – which is passing from one state to another. Isn't this what we want? To find the way to move from depression or any "negative" state to another more positive one? Releasing and detaching is the answer to freedom. Letting go of the disappointment, expectation, and loss makes room to create and give birth to new "forms" in your life. It then becomes possible to find a new normal and live the way you want, or create a version of your dreams you didn't imagine before.

When you let unhealthy things within you die, you create the fertile soil to grow and express new parts of yourself. Often, we are stubborn and need to marinate in this dark place to breakdown inner barriers for things to become clear. Sometimes it's a matter of getting "sick of being me" that forces a breakthrough into a lighter place.

Like my client Ed, who was desperate for something to change. He'd been laid off six months earlier and couldn't land a job. Interviews went nowhere, and then opportunities disappeared altogether. As the weeks went on and his bank account diminished he became deeply depressed, making his situation look and feel even worse.

Being stuck home alone for months had created a "dark night" to look at all the anger he carried for years before the layoff. And a chance for him to look at how he denied and underemployed his creative talents he'd ditched in favor of analytical work to pay the bills. Unemployment was an opportunity forcing him to confront and clear energy and emotions piling up to an intolerable level. He reached out to me for help.

Although he didn't want to admit it, he was angry at his last employer, at his situation, and most of all angry at himself. He believed he was discriminated against in the workplace because of his "size." He is a big guy who for years used food to medicate himself against childhood trauma. But suppressing and ignoring his feelings wasn't working. His anger leaked out in his demeanor, and more so in his energy field, where I saw it creating a jagged edge that others could feel and avoided without knowing why. It kept people away, just as he intended, but now it threatened his livelihood. He could no longer hide this "edge" to his personality behind a shy demeanor, or contain it with food, or convince himself it was other people's problem for not understanding his quirky personality. It was time to look at what he was holding on to on all levels.

During a session, we talked about how he hid from his feelings, while I psychically helped him move and shift the energy field around him. As the barrier between him and his body changed, he could feel the darkness hiding beneath the depression. He tapped into the anger and pain of his isolation, and with nothing left to shield him, sensed the small young man desperate for acceptance who just wanted to paint, have fun and be silly without being judged. Hearing and feeling the truth, he wept for the first time in years.

Ed later told me that from that point on he felt calmer and less angry about everything in his life. What's more, he experienced a definite change externally. Within days of our conversation, two friends who did not know each other and who he hadn't talked to in months reached out and suggested that he apply to their companies. He also received a call from a recruiter and was offered a position he happily accepted.

Waking up to the things that want or need to pass away can be frightening. Like a snake that's outgrown its skin, we're forced to shed old beliefs and relationships we let define us. We release identities that no longer work. And like a snake, there is a time between the world of the old and the new when we are most vulnerable and unsure. We are exposed. It is a place of not knowing what's next, not knowing what to do.

What is the dark trying to teach you? Now is the time to enter in and ask.

What in your life is no longer working? Have you settled for less than you want? Have you allowed yourself to make do because you think it's all you can have? Do you give up your opinion or ideas to keep things quiet and calm? These things grate on us, adding to the deadness inside.

Do you hold on to the past by reliving what should or could have been? Are you holding on to old beliefs just to be "right?" Do you deny reality by refusing to accept what is? Holding on to what needs to die eventually turns against you. These thoughts and emotions fester and create stagnant energy that can turn into physical illness and disease.

The following chapters will guide you to recognize and use the dark to transition to a lighter, happier life. You'll learn to wait patiently in the dark, staying open to what comes. With willingness and trust, let the Universe meet you in support.

Chapter 5

WALK BETWEEN WORLDS

When you are open and vulnerable, you become present. In that presence is power. If you're willing, you see signs not noticed before; pushed by magic and guided by grace. It takes all of your senses and heightened awareness. Being in between worlds feels like longing and remembering. It's floating in not knowing; not needing to know.

When you're in between worlds, ordinary life doesn't hold much interest or meaning. Routines and logic stop working. To-do lists, structure, and reason serve only to tighten the stranglehold of confusion. What used to make sense makes no sense at all. It doesn't matter how much you ask why or how, no simple answer comes back. It's not until you leap off into the unknown that meaning takes shape in chaos.

Repeatedly I've been broken open by life and plummeted into despair. But each time it's when I surrender to walking between worlds and fill my darkness with things that want to belong there that I shift. Light makes its way through the cracks when I let go.

Many times, I find it in the words of poets and writers who capture some hidden part of me I can't see and reflect it back. I'm rescued from the depths by another's words that send a shiver of truth through my body, like a hammer to a gong; reverberating and lifting my spirit even if I do not understand why.

Digging in the garden, doodling aimlessly, playing with crayons and a coloring book – these are all ways I float in between worlds without thinking and knowing. Just letting myself "be" in dreamy, or seemingly pointless activity allows the light to inch its way in.

I slip between worlds in Nature, or Nature finds me, like an insistent bird tapping at my window, or a feather floating down from the sky at the exact moment I'm wondering "am I on the right path?" On a fateful trip to North Carolina during the fall, a ladybug (a sign of good luck) appeared out of nowhere on the wall in my hotel room, then showed up again two days later in my cabin over a hundred miles away. Bears have crossed my path out of the blue twice in the wild, one a collision, one a conversation. (I'll talk more about this later.)

To see in the dark requires extraordinary vision like a nocturnal animal making its way at night, able to spot what for others is impossible to see. Searching in a dark place in your life requires the same vision to find the creatures within that don't show up in the light of day, to hunt in the shadows and discover that even though it looks scary, there is so much life and wisdom there.

The Owl who comes alive in the dark has long been a favorite of mine. I used to hear it some nights outside my window as a child. It frightened me with its plaintive call followed by the dying shrieks of its prey, but its presence thrilled me as a symbol of wisdom and spoke to my longing to always know more. The owl is a companion to the goddess Athena, the goddess of the night, and sits on her shoulder to whisper hidden truths in her ear. Owl took me on a deep dive into the Dark once to a place that even now as I relate this story, I don't understand.

I was in my early 30s and visiting my family back in Kansas. As always, I slept in my former bedroom that hadn't changed in years. It was another stressful visit during that time of my life as I struggled to heal the sexual abuse I experienced as a child. I was contemplating telling my father about what happened at the hands of his friend, and some in my family didn't want me bringing up the past. The pressure was on to keep things quiet from both inside and outside me.

One night during that visit, I lay in bed nearly asleep when I heard the low, constant "who – who – whooo" outside my window. It was close and loud. It was insistent. Instead of comforting me as it once would, I was unnerved. I got up and walked out to the living room to search for the bird out the big windows lining the back wall of the house. The backyard lamp and a silvery moon cast enough light to see most of the barren tree branches. Nothing.

I returned to my room hoping for quiet, and the chance to sleep but the Owl called out before I reached my door. Just then my mother emerged from her room down the dark hallway.

"Do you hear that owl?" I said. "It's keeping me awake."

She looked at me dreamily and didn't respond. She seemed to float out to the kitchen.

"Turn on the backyard light," she said and went back to her room, leaving me wondering if she was even awake. Was she an apparition, like the elusive owl outside my window?

Finally, anger kicked in. I had to see this damn owl and scare it off if I was to have any peace. I left my room again and went to the mudroom where I donned my father's big work coat and pulled on my mother's gardening shoes. Out in the backyard now I stopped and listened for my tormentor, breathing in the cold night air, noticing the frost sparkling on the dead grass.

"Whoooo, who," it called far to my right from the tree outside my bedroom window. I walked to the tree, peering up into the dark branches, looking for but now dreading seeing its glowing eyes. I was almost under the tree when I heard it call again. But this time it came from the tree closest to where I'd stood initially, just off the patio. I spun around and headed back. Again, the closer I got to the source the sound shifted, now coming from a tree further back in the yard near the fence. Back and forth I walked until I had a strange sense of being watched. I felt foolish as if someone pulled a joke to get me outside and I fell for it.

Okay, you won. You got me out here. The moment I thought it, the calls stopped.

Something from the dark was calling me and wanted me outside. I felt it profoundly but wasn't sure why or what I was supposed to do. I feared what might come next. If I look Darkness in the face and speak the truth, what will happen? I might be snatched up at any moment, never to return.

I ran back into the house, stripped off my parent's clothes and rushed for the warmth of my bed. Once there, the storm windows above my headboard vibrated with a low hum, sounding nothing like the familiar rattle caused by the Kansas wind that lulled me to sleep over the years. This was rapid and steady. I put my hand on the window to stop it, but it continued. I then put my right hand on the wall, and it too vibrated and shook.

Again, I felt dumbfounded. What is happening? How can mom and dad sleep through this?

Then it stopped as suddenly as it began. Shaken and far too awake for sleep, I pulled out a notebook and wrote down what had just happened. I didn't know what it meant. I still wasn't sure it was real.

In the years since, I understand that "true" or not, real or not, it was my experience, and that it is true for me to walk between worlds, to navigate the dark places and find wisdom there. When I confronted the terrifying shadow hanging over my life and talked about the abuse of my past, many dark places rose up with it. It's as if the psychic soup of everyone involved came together to scare me off, to hash it out, and give me a chance to face the dark to clear it out of my life. That night gave me a taste of the magical world I know exists in all of us, for all of us where the spiritual and physical collide. It is the place of medicine women and shamans, of philosophers and prophets. It takes a trained eye and a courageous heart to go there, even more so to stay and learn.

Standing alone in the cold night, I felt a godly presence watching me through that bird's eyes and sensed a voice from deep inside me calling to look beyond the small walls of my childhood, and the narrow path imposed by abuse, depression, and alcoholism. I understand it now as a call to remember my divinity and the wisdom and potential waiting for me beyond a thinly veiled wall of limited daily perceptions. *Just open the door and step into your power.*

Strange things happen to all of us. If we are lucky enough to notice the signs, life can pivot down another path, opening to vistas that we were once too small-minded to imagine. In this place, no logic or rational thinking can help. It needs a different mind.

If life continues to make little sense to you, stop asking "why am I unhappy?" Stop telling yourself the same story in explanation. When you're between worlds, the old rules don't apply. Look elsewhere. Look to myth and symbol, to nature. Immerse yourself in music or language. Get out of synch with time.

When I let the mundane, trivial things fall away and slip into this other place, my senses become heightened as I pay close attention to what shows up in my surroundings. I notice the type and timing of things and people as I stay open to being in the world in a new way. A word or idea pops into my mind that feels helpful, then a stranger mentions the same thing in passing the next day. Later, seemingly to drive the point home, a random click of the TV remote shows me an interview discussing exactly what I needed to hear. When I stop trying to solve problems in my mind, synchronicities abound. What I need shows up, what I don't need falls away without effort.

In the temporary place between worlds, connections are lost and created. You fall away from friends and family – pull into yourself to find the connections to ancestors locked in your bones that you'd forgotten. Memories stir. If you get quiet and go inside yourself to contemplate you can ask the Spirits of those before you to help light the way. It takes trust. It's risky – this sudden shift from reality into something bigger, but it's needed to get answers in a new way.

Einstein, another highly intuitive introvert said you can't solve a problem with the same consciousness that created it. A new consciousness is the "between worlds" place. The place of night dreams and daydreams, detached from material things and doing, and instead settling into being. What does "being" look like? Many things – watching rain roll down a window, listening to the soft breath of your sleeping child, feeling a shaft of sunlight warming your skin.

Shifting consciousness into this place is like seeing an invisible thread of spider silk strung from a tree branch to its trunk caught suddenly by sunlight and reflected. What hid in plain sight appears. You observe the thing that connects disparate objects – the light linking heaven and earth – and glimpse Spirit moving in the wind. That is the place between worlds – where the unseen illuminates, connecting our split self. Meaning and truth flood in, impossible to articulate, and with it comes a broad sense of wholeness. You are home again in the largeness of things.

Chapter 6

CREATIVITY

Just as a baby or seed incubates in the darkness, when its time has come, the push toward the light is inevitable. There's no holding back this creative force running deeply in each one of us. Nature, which includes us, exists to let life come through. It is our instinct to survive.

Simply being alive is a creative act. Our bodies continue to grow, multiply and recreate at a cellular level, no matter how stuck and uncreative we might feel. Even the Universe, as we know now, is always expanding. Our intended state of beingness allows creativity to flow through us – a state of consciousness – that propels life forward without thought. Aware or not, like it or not, you are a creative being, and this same creative force wants to come through you.

Creativity is not only artistic talent, musical genius, or scientific brilliance, it's everything on a spectrum from the mundane to miraculous insights. Whether it's wearing colorful scarves to work every day, rebuilding an old car engine, baking fancy cupcakes for school events, or decorating every inch of your yard at Christmas, creative expression is essential to a happy life.

Because it is often insistent and seemingly endless, it's easy to misinterpret the urge of creative energy as something to calm, silence or completely shut down. The consequence of this, however, is that creative energy held back feels like anxiety and restlessness. It's the leg that won't stop bouncing when you sit at your desk, or it's biting your fingernails unconsciously or eating even if you're not hungry.

Depression is also a sign of repressed creative energy. We find ourselves turning to addictive or numbing behaviors like sleep, watching TV, or playing video games for hours to keep our unbridled creativity under control. But be aware if you ignore the unique expression of who you are and what you love, it turns on you, spiraling inward like a dangerous trapped beauty. Life, in the form of creative expression, gnaws at you. It's held back and wants out.

We suffer when we get out of flow with this creative force, and each of us needs to connect, realign, and then express creative life force in whatever way feels right to us and is uniquely ours.

Instead of crumbling under the weight of creative energy pushing us toward expansion and growth we can open to it and intentionally become a broader, deeper channel for this life force to flow through us. We do that by being more of our Self.

When we stop fighting our nature, ease comes. My friend Jennifer suffered bouts of deep depression and anxiety for years, often because she expected to have a "real career" and work up the corporate ladder despite her inward personality. Or she spent too much time and energy volunteering or organizing outings for friends, putting pressure on herself to be more social, make others happy, and not let anyone down. If she was honest with herself, all she wanted was to be at home, quietly gardening and raising wildly colored chickens and collecting their pastel eggs.

At first, Jennifer criticized her lack of business drive as she did more of what made her feel good. But eventually, she let go of obligations and retired from work altogether, making her health and peace of mind her full-time job. By being herself and doing what she loves, she's created a sanctuary on a busy street where neighbors and passing strangers alike stop to pick a juicy orange or smell the roses climbing over the fence. Delighted toddlers talk to the chickens pecking furiously at the ground, giving a new mom a moment to breathe. Jennifer grows delicious organic vegetables and sends out email blasts inviting the neighbors to share in the harvest. She adds sounds, smells, color and life to everything she does. Jennifer has done more for the world around her by doing what her larger self calls her to do than she could ever have done in corporate life by letting creative energy flow through her and doing the things she loves to do. Her work has value and people appreciate her. She's leaving her mark; others will remember her. She teaches me daily as I pass by her house that following our nature, and being connected to Nature, is a healing path.

Her selfless nature has found a way to care for her too. I recently caught her lovingly tending the soil around three sunflower plants that popped up on their own in a desolate bit of dirt near the sidewalk. She smiled as she worked, thinking about the bright yellow flowers to come. But what she really loves, she said, is knowing that when others drive past and see the sunny faces, they might smile too.

Viewing the darkness of depression as creative potential opens us up to healing. Many times, I've built a ladder out of the pit by turning to a mindless creative act to sidestep my pain. Something as simple as doodling rows of spirals that never end or sitting in the dirt making impromptu sculptures from the scattered bits of nature shifts my mood. I'm no longer where I was when I started. Some hidden part of me arrives. It's been waiting in my subconscious, those thoughts and feelings that exist inside the mind influencing behavior though I'm unaware, looking for a channel to express itself. As it comes through, my desire to figure things out or control anything disappears. I find peace.

The subconscious has gotten a bad rap for years in the field of psychology, thanks to the founding father Sigmund Freud who deemed it the source of neuroses and psychosis. But it's also how we store and remember everything we've ever experienced. Our subconscious is where genius and insight spring from. Where the ideas, art, and visions that leap to mind and propel humanity forward allow creativity to flow through and express in new forms. This "other mind" is a limitless source providing answers to problems both big and small through intuition and inspiration. It's a new way of seeing, knowing, and comprehending what is possible beyond the present moment's understanding.

Creative expression is an opportunity to line up with this other, vast part of you. It opens the bottleneck of energy, ideas, thoughts, and emotions, so life flows through you instead of feeling like it's something that happens to you.

How do you let your neglected creative expression appear? Start with your body. Slow down, turn your attention inward. Breathe. Ask what wants to come through. The more you tune into your body, the more your creative instincts will rise. Pay attention, be spontaneous.

And, the more you allow creative life force to express through you, the more your intuition, that direct knowing without knowing how you know, pours through to solve problems, inspire, and reveal who you are and what matters to you. There are answers to things the logical mind can't resolve that flow with ease through creative activity.

Creativity is a doorway to the place between worlds. It's these darker places where inspiration and ideas come from. The dark is the source of the light.

Often, nothing in the outside world can reach our sadness because it isn't there. It lives in a different space/time – in an energy wound of the past, or in the emotional pain of others we unknowingly heal in our energy field. We can't hand it off to another, bury it, brush it off. Our sadness wants us to meet where it lives – inside, deep in the shadows – and creativity is a doorway to do that.

Creativity is the place of fairy tales and science fiction, fantasy and otherworldliness. It is between worlds. Unhooking from the logical mind by getting lost in a project or movement puts you in a state of flow where time stops or expands, breathing slows, the mind wanders, and nothing else is important.

When I'm open to being physically different in the world, the door cracks open to this other place. In an altered state of creative energy, I hear, see, and then more easily move the weight of depression pinning me down. As the weight moves, the door opens even more and allows creative energy through. My body and mood are lightened. What is hidden in the dark is revealed.

Often, I can't look depression straight in the eyes, like Medusa, so I find her when I shift out of my mind and paint my feelings on a canvas – stormy seas and skies, a twister heading straight for me. She's found when I blast native American chants in my ears, drums, and voices reverberating through my belly and bones. I call her out when I let my pen flow vitriolic or with terrified whispers instead of trying to quiet her truth.

The old ones knew, and know, it is the circle, the fire, the song, and the dance that holds the dark places for us all. They found and healed wounds and worries here when body and spirit meet.

Moving from mere moments of creative consciousness to longer stretches of grounded appreciation and connectedness is living happy, with depression. The goal is to lengthen, widen, and deepen that road through creativity, and pay whole-hearted attention to whatever moment I'm in. Like now as I write, rather than cursing the noisy gardener next door distracting me from my work, I focus on his whistling and tap into the tune of his heart. The chainsaw he wields? That's a tougher challenge to take on. But that is the practice.

Chapter 7

THE CREATIVE CYCLE

When my daughters became teenagers and the demands of carpools and caretaking diminished, I enlisted the help of a business mentor to expand my consulting practice. It was a challenge to extricate myself from family routines and budget more time for me and my work because my habit is always to put family first. With fits and starts, I saw progress. But over time our phone calls turned from discussing what I'd accomplished toward meeting my business goals and what was next, to how to stop stopping and get back on track with my work. My mentor used the phrase "creative cycle" as we talked about yet another of my downturns in enthusiasm and income, hoping I'd acknowledge there might be a natural flow to how I operate impacting my work.

Like everyone, I had good times and bad times. There was a pattern to my behavior that seemed to take me from high and low and back again. In a blatant instance of timing, something clicked in me. I realized that regardless of the outside circumstances of my life, I come back to depression over and over in the same way. To change this pattern, I had first to understand what the hell it is. I had to see it in some form outside myself that I could grasp.

Inspired in that moment of realization, I grabbed crayons and paper and drew a shaky circle. The symbol felt right because this cycle keeps me going in circles. I asked myself, "What is it I do and feel? What is the path I keep going down? Is there some sense in the chaos of my unruly emotions?"

As I pushed the crayon around and around, I thought "What if this is just a rhythm, my rhythm, a true cycle I can regulate, ride, enjoy and understand? What is my way? What are my needs as I circle around and around from high to low places and everywhere in between? How do I empower myself through it knowing I do not live or die in any single place? That I am not stuck in one place in this ever-evolving cycle and can accept that having a bad day doesn't mean I've failed or I am a failure. How do I own all parts of this cycle and let myself slide into the quiet, dark places and come back out whole?"

Although it was a creative act that got me to understand it, the "creative cycle" is not about making art. By creative, I mean expansive, open – connected to the energy that wants to come through you and drives toward life, growth, and survival – just as in all of nature. It is an opening seed that sprouts roots and forces shoots up through the dirt and dark surrounding it despite crappy circumstances. When you live creatively, you are dynamic, curious. You seek to know more and find discovery of any kind fascinating.

What's more, the Creative Cycle is what it takes to get you underground to the vital dark place that's a natural process of life. Our human intelligence and arrogance allow us to forget that we are animals, part of Nature and all its cycles moving in and around us. From the grand scale of being born, maturing and dying, to the annual seasons turning within that lifetime. The monthly path of the moon, and the daily rise and fall of the sun and with it our emotional life that ebbs and flows according to myriad circumstances. Cycles within cycles impact us as we walk through life unaware.

We have good days; we have bad days. Navigating changes to our day is easier by understanding and respecting our animal rhythm, tied to nature at a cellular level, responding to the Earth and everyone around us. Embracing this rhythm expands our vision as part of the larger world.

As I looked for a pattern leading to depression, I could've drawn a ladder of emotions that took me straight down to the pit. But I was more interested in figuring out that bit of light that would start me back up on the upward trend. More importantly, how can I learn to sling-shot my way around the long curve of darker emotions and get myself up in the Light faster? Here's how my cycle looks.

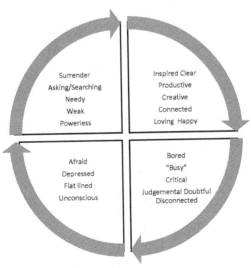

I envision the segments of my Creative Cycle as Light, Waning, Dark, and Waxing. They are perpetual like the Moon building to the full and then receding to darkness. For years, I've noted the cycle of the moon above me, to plant seeds of intention at the new moon like the ancient farmers, then at the full moon harvest the rewards of my work or let go of things that died. An endless and powerful cycle covering the spectrum of light and dark.

I appreciate this lunar quality inside me. I like seeing my cycle in physical form and having seen it, I am ready to imagine a new one that draws on the power of the darkness to create rather than staying stuck.

There are so many clues about how to change in Waning; my mind is too busy, I'm doing without thinking and rushing from one task to the next. It's hard to relax or sit still. I feel like doing "something" but don't know what it is. I'm pacing, restless, and bored, and mindlessly eating even if I'm not hungry.

How do I stop the downward slide around the circle? My body is the answer. I'm not paying attention! Deep breathing is enough to get me started. When I take a deep breath, I sense my body from the inside out. I notice where I'm holding tension, where things hurt. I realize I am thirsty, tired or hungry. I hear a small voice behind the blustery one of judgment and anger that says she needs attention.

So, beginning the descent, there is a need to be taken care of that is at the core of it all. I determine what I need at the moment and come through for myself. Maybe it's asking my husband or the girls to make dinner and clean up, or just walking away from my to-do list and taking a nap. Noticing myself at this point is critical because my habit, which is just an ingrained pattern, is to pull back from the world, and recede into the rising negative thoughts and the tension that comes with it. I mentally build a case for why I'm right about all the horrible things I think about my life are correct and look for ways to prove it. Proof then shows up around me because wherever I put my energy and attention is what I receive. Our outer world reflects our inner world.

So, the trick at the first sign of descent for me now is to stay connected and to say what I want out loud. It can be something as simple as saying to my family, "I'm feeling restless right now and don't know what to do. Would you go for a walk with me?"

Or I cuddle up on the sofa next to my husband without a word instead of bitching at him to "turn off the damn TV." I stop my girls in the hallway and hug them. I call a friend I know will understand when I say I don't like myself at the moment and I want to stop feeling bad.

I know I need beauty when I'm in this waning place. I need movement. A simple grocery store bouquet or a walk around the block will suffice. And, I need to settle down and feel whatever I'm feeling. When I'm in that place, is the time I need to cry. Sometimes I must find a sad movie to help myself weep.

***

Yes, it's possible to stop the descent through willingness – an awkward, uncomfortable new territory somewhere between the next step further into familiar negativity and not exactly jumping for joy. It's a neutral emotional netherworld inviting change without knowing how it will look or feel and teaches us how to be vulnerable.

What I find underneath all the boredom and bitchiness showing up before getting depressed is a small part of me who wants to cry like a cranky child. I want someone, somewhere to make things "better," even though I do not understand who or what.

It's a good time to look back to find any thoughts that set me off. I felt good just two weeks ago so what changed? Usually, I can recall a little disappointment, an unmet expectation. I'd hoped or dreamed something, and it didn't go as I planned. My habit is so ingrained that I make even the smallest problem or setback proof of my failure, instead of just accepting the situation or looking for a way through. Somewhere in the far recesses of my mind was the "nothing works out" or "I'm just not good enough at this" voice. It was so quiet, so subtle and familiar, that I missed it.

Being neutral and willing wakes you up to see the lifelines being thrown by friends, family or the Universe, reminding you what is good and full of potential. Softer, hopeful voices fill your mind, and you're free to hear the welcoming sound of birdsong, a favorite song or laughter. You can let yourself be just OK. That's big; to be ok with being ok. And then the cycle upward begins in baby steps or giant leaps or anything in between, it doesn't matter, but the more you pay attention and are willing the faster it goes.

And there is within this cycle of light and dark a necessary solitude; the dark moon time that is reflective, meditative, introspective. It is a time of quiet and replenishing, especially for sensitive people, that makes it possible to go back into the world at all.

There are different types of dark within the creative cycle, and as I embrace less appealing emotions, I find that spending quality introspective time with them in the first place keeps their visit short. The reluctance to be alone and wholeheartedly entertain our darkness keeps us high strung or run down and susceptible to gloom and giving up. We need to let our inner world gestate without the glare of expectation and engagement.

Now I have a new Creative Cycle because I understand:

1. that I have one and
2. that all parts of it are useful, so
3. the Dark Moon part of it is reflective.

In that reflective time, I feel sad, angry, disappointed or whatever emotion that would typically take me to my knees and work with it. I give it time but in the right way with space and quiet, so I can go down and come back. I skip past languishing in despair and "not knowing what to do" and move right back into the light.

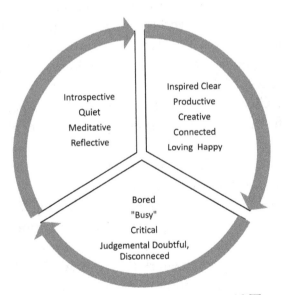

It is all about paying attention to myself. That is the bottom line. If I intend to listen and learn, then my awareness will take me through and back up toward expansion and creativity instead of imploding or retracting emotionally by escaping or denying how I feel. Intention gives awareness direction.

I find new strength to act on my behalf and the action, no matter how small, that moves me in a positive direction becomes possible. I see it, do it, then give myself credit for what I've done.

What is my Creative Cycle? It is the round and around rhythm transitioning me internally from hope and light to darkness and despair and everything in between. It used to plod in big, slow circles over time like Saturn's orbit moving from dark to light over the years. As I opened to my spiritual self, the cycle became months, then weeks. Now it is just days, and sometimes only hours.

Lost days of darkness, instead of lost years. That's realistic, that's human. That's who I want to be. A woman who navigates both worlds and finds the gifts in them. A woman who stays AWAKE and attentive to my feelings, thoughts, body and my energy vibration as much as my willingness allows.

The Creative Cycle exercise altered the perspective of my life. Before, it was like standing in the center of a loud merry-go-round watching crazy colored lights and carousel animals spin around me as I pray to get off, believing I need someone else to cut the power.

Now, life is more like standing above a big Wheel of Fortune that I get to spin. I see all the options there before me, some good, some not, but every day is a new spin, and I'll give it a whirl. I know now I can decide if I like what lands in front of me. If not, I can choose to spin again and pick up something else.

Here is the truth: I am all of this. There are gifts in all.

Your Creative Cycle

Write feelings or words that capture where you are at

this moment, where you've just come from, and where you usually go from here. Do these looks and sound familiar? Do some feelings seem to hang out together and get lumped into different sections? Notice feelings that transition you from one place to the next. There is no right answer. It's just an exploration.

Write the first things that pop into your mind. Leave your words for a while and come back to see if it still feels right and edit from there. You know yourself well by now, so the first thoughts are accurate. Jot side notes about what pushes or pulls you to a segment and what brings you out. How willing would you be to stop the slide down the circle? How willing are you right now to be OK?

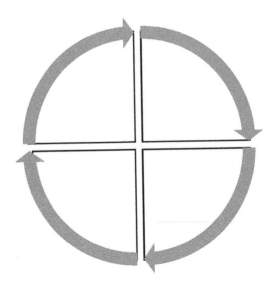

Chapter 8

SHUT UP AND LISTEN

When life throws her a problem, Elizabeth rushes in to fix it. She gets serious and focused, and angry as she tells herself that if she'd done everything right, she wouldn't have problems. Mistakes, setbacks, or life challenges mean she's done something "wrong." She acts fast to cover her tracks, to find out if there is someone else to blame and to make things right as quickly as possible. Once in problem-solving mode, the blinders are on. She finds fault in everything and everybody.

Deep in critical thoughts, all that negativity poses as positive thinking. Elizabeth finds what's not working, what's left to do. All the things she could change. But inside it feeds her failure. She can't rest. She can't let others rest either, always asking her family, "Have you done this, what is your plan, can you do more?" On and on the critical thoughts build to a crescendo that turns to white noise.

She can't hear the stories she tells herself and no longer listens to her feelings. She ignores what her body tries to tell her as she overeats and works too hard. Eventually, what she hears is this: I'm sick. Sick of my life. Nothing will ever change.

Thoughts are things. They lead us places we don't want to go when we have an unfavorable view of ourselves and the world. The power of our thoughts is real, but so is our ability to change them.

Listening to ourselves builds the bridge of awareness we need to take us from madness to miracles when life feels hard. It keeps us from falling into despair. Actively listening is a new awareness of ourselves. It means paying attention and noticing what you experience from the inside, out.

For me, the framework for that bridge was in my thoughts, where I discovered how much of what I was thinking fueled my negative emotions. However, as an intuitive, noticing my feelings is equally significant – who or what is influencing how I feel? Feelings can also come first and drive thoughts.

The bridge grows longer and wider as we learn to tune into and listen to our body for information and guidance. It's here that awareness expands to include a direct connection with our highest spiritual wisdom and a deeper understanding of our life.

We'll start with listening to our thoughts. Many fields of study accept that emotions are a response to what we think. If you pay attention, you'll notice that much of what goes through your mind is the same thing every day. When we think the same way, we will feel the same, so paying attention to thoughts is crucial to changing our emotional state. If we're caught in a negative loop of thinking, like feeling as if we're not enough, our feelings and experiences constantly replay, keeping us stuck in the problem and attracting more of the same. Remember the universal law like attracts like?

If you're like me, you tend toward negative thinking, whether it's your personality, experience, or just the fault of your stars. But it is in part due to our nature. The mind is tied to our primitive brain that helped us survive as a species over thousands of years. We are hard-wired to remember danger, so we run for our life or stand and fight. The tendency to remember bad stuff is an encoded program that runs without us even realizing it, like breathing. We don't think about it; it happens as part of the autonomic nervous system. That's why we need attention and awareness to reveal and then shift where our thoughts go.

Our thoughts are like layers of currents passing through our mind, most of which go unnoticed. We catch the ones on the surface, the loudest, the usual. But it's the deeper, faster ones that pull us under into the emotional depths. The noise we don't hear, the thought behind the thought.

The next time you face a challenge or an uncomfortable social interaction, slow down and listen to what you say to yourself as you think about the situation. Are you judgmental, whiny, or mean? What do you tell yourself about you? How many times do you use exaggerated, statements like "I never..." or "he always..." that simply aren't true? What is the conversation going on in your mind? Is the voice you hear the "real" you?

When you listen to your thoughts, you'll notice the various voices, like characters in a play, dictating how you feel. How you're talking to yourself in your head makes all the difference in your experience. When I listen with intent, I most often hear one of two "voices" that keep me from moving forward in creating the life I want and feeling happy with the life I have. There's a difference in the tone of voice of my thoughts: one is the critic, one is just lazy.

We're all familiar with the critical inner voice but may not realize how it runs a constant loop commenting on our experience. We direct it at others by slinging judgment, or at ourselves in a deluge of comparison to figure out how we measure up. Criticism keeps us stuck, caught in a tar pit of untruths based on old beliefs or experiences that have nothing to do with the present moment.

Catching these thoughts gives you an opportunity to step back and question what you're hearing. It is the time to go easy on yourself. Are you realistic about your expectations of yourself? Is all the negative crap you're telling yourself about yourself true? Our thoughts get locked into a fictional version of ourselves, muddying our worldview with untruth that colors our experience.

No one is crueler to us than ourselves. How often is your inner voice calling you names? Just listen, we all do it. Then stand up to your critical, inner bully and say, "Enough! I don't want to feel like this; I don't have to. None of this is true." Treat yourself like someone you like or love, even if you don't believe it at the moment, and change the thought.

Consider the tone of your thoughts and words and talk to yourself like you would a friend or loved one who has the same issue, problem, or concern as you. If you can't feel loving, then at least try to be as kind as you would be to a stranger in distress. If being kind isn't possible, then reach for being realistic. When you hear yourself using a lot of black and white thinking words – like always, never, or only – you're simply not telling yourself the truth. That's the trap of "either – or" thinking. You're either this way or that way and nothing in between. There is no gray area for compromise or creativity for something new to be true.

On a bad day, I can effortlessly ride a train of thought until I'm convinced I've accomplished nothing of merit. Or, that I'm not talented, disciplined, or intelligent enough and I'll never meet a goal – like losing weight or saving for that dream trip. I'll never finish my writing projects. Never? Really? Haven't I done these things in varying degrees in the past? I am capable of it, I've done it and can do it again. Here's when giving myself credit at the moment is crucial. I challenge that complaining, insulting voice and remind myself of the truth. For instance, I might fail to meet my writing deadline on a particular day, but it doesn't make me a failure. I've met my goals before and have both failed and succeeded overall.

Or for example, I'm conveying my thoughts as a teacher as I write this book, which also makes me a student learning a new and more detailed way to communicate. Both aspects are real in different ways at different times. Both are true at the same time. I recognize that I don't have to know it all and stop judging myself for doing something I've never done before perfectly the first time around. Learning the truth of "both-and" has freed me from black and white, either-or thinking. It gives me room to grow, to breathe – the space to be OK.

When you listen, you'll also notice those thoughts that unconsciously make you give up or forget what you want. For example, I went for a walk in keeping with my desire to be healthy. About halfway up the hill, I told myself I didn't need to walk to the top. "I can cut it short. I've already done a lot this morning. Besides, I want to spend time at the creek. It's getting late, and it's hotter than I thought. I don't need to overdo it. I'll just stop at the next hill and turn back..."

It sounds like a logical, caring voice – it makes so much sense, right? But the voice of these thoughts puts me to sleep, makes me stop when things get tougher, and keeps me from completing. It sounds like justified laziness really – it's the voice of Excuses. And as helpful and logical as that voice sounds, it keeps me from striving hard enough to complete my goals, even though I'm a hard worker. That's when I need to be "hard" on myself in a good way. "No, don't give up. You want this; you can do this. Do the hard thing because it makes you stronger. You'll be so proud when you do!"

I call this my coach voice – it's clear, matter of fact, and focused in tone and feeling. Notice too how my thoughts shift perspective – from saying "I" (who wants an easy way out) to a positive, strong voice saying "you" can do it.

Be the coach. Don't give up. At first, this resilient voice might sound like a taskmaster urging you to get up, try again, keep going, or let go, but as you learn to listen you discover that it's not hard on you. This voice isn't condemning or judging. It speaks to who you want to be, who you really are.

For years I secretly worried that I was not very "conscious" because using affirmations didn't work for me. I know now I needed to understand what it was I was telling myself in the first place and not just cover it up with a band-aid of positivity. Saying affirmations felt phony because the thought behind the thought was running in the background, taking up space and setting the tone for my day.

The tone of our thoughts is essential, just as the tone we take in our spoken conversations, so listen to your attitude and perspective. For example, I check myself when I think about projects and commitments. Do I see them as a grim to-do list, or do I think, "I can't wait to get back to it. I'm so lucky to work doing what I love." When I chat with friends, do I complain and give them a "poor me" rundown on what's not going right with family obligations and work, or do I say, "I'm proud of myself for working hard. I'm so excited that things are going well?"

In her book *Mindset, The New Psychology of Success*,[1] author Carol Dweck details the differences between the critic and the coach mental frameworks that determine our level of success and happiness, calling them a fixed (judge-and-be-judged) versus growth (learn-and-help-learn) mindset. Dweck's work complements a spiritual view of unlimited potential, underscores our capacity for learning based on brain science, and proves we are not limited by what we know. We can change because we continually learn. This is great news! Understanding how our mindset works will show us we are not limited by our thoughts, feelings or actions if we put in the work to learn. How we think is a framework that can be broken down and rebuilt anew.

Our perspective widens to see how much is available for us, and rather than falling back in depressed defeat at what we don't know or can't do we revel in the chance to learn more.

Distinguishing the truth of what we tell ourselves makes all the difference between moving forward in life or staying stuck. Life is often challenging – dealing with setbacks, growing, and changing requires work. It was a welcome relief realizing that I don't have to take it personally or make it mean something bad about me when life is hard, or I make mistakes. Whatever I experience in these situations depends on the story I choose to tell myself.

Cultivating awareness through listening lets us come to what's called radical acceptance – which is being able to accept at a deep level that touches us in our heart, soul, and mind. It means recognizing that reality is what it is rather than denying and wishing for things to be the way we want. It means accepting the truth, and, allowing that life is worth living even with the pain.

Acceptance doesn't mean we agree, or condone, or give up, but it focuses events and situations in an accurate light, allowing anger, self-hate, depression, anxiety and more to decrease as the thoughts driving negative feelings begin to diminish. Overwhelm and apathy drain away. What follows is the ability to see honestly what can be done. What change is within our power? The one thing we can always change is how we respond to situations and others' behavior. Now is when taking small actions and giving ourselves credit for what moves us forward comes into play. These are the nails that hold the bridge of awareness together as we extend it plank by plank.

Pay attention to yourself by listening to your thoughts and words. Show kindness when you need it, buckle down and push yourself in a positive direction to learn and grow when it's a must.

Chapter 9

HOW TO LISTEN

As with any structure, the bridge to a deeper awareness of fleeting thoughts and emotions needs a foundation. Our body anchors that foundation. Shifting attention to our physical reality changes our experience. We tend to "live in our head," caught up in our mind with thinking, planning, and doing. We fall prey to those repeated thoughts that drive us unconsciously. As a result, we ignore the sensations our body gives us about our feelings and health. We miss the physical clues about the energy we pick up, hold, and reflect.

Being present in your physical body lets you know yourself in a new way. Your body becomes the doorway to a rich inner world where you can seek help and find answers from your intuition, the authoritative voice of your Soul when aligned with your Spirit.

What's it like to drop out of your head and into your body? It's the difference between standing outside your home describing what it looks and feels like versus stepping inside and sitting on the furniture, smelling the food cooking on the stove, running your feet over the carpet.

The furniture may be plush or stiff, the food acrid from burning or delightful, the carpet soft or scratchy. But you must be inside to truly experience the environment and know what you want to keep or change.

How do you get through the door? Breath is best.

We take our breath for granted and give it little thought. Notice it now. As you do, your attention drops out of your mind and goes immediately to your nose and chest. You feel space expand inside your ribs. In an instant, your perspective has changed.

Notice how much air you take in. Most of us breathe far too shallow, robbing our bodies of oxygen and movement. Breath animates us. It is proof of life. The simple act of closing our eyes and taking a deep breath is enough to shift awareness out of our head. It's an instant "meditation" practice that can be built upon to notice and manage how we feel daily. It gives us a solid foundation to stand on when choosing how we think and feel.

When I ask new clients if they meditate, inevitably they squirm in their seat. Meditation is an intimidating subject that convinces most people they can't do it. But trust me when I say it doesn't require perfection. It is not achieving a holy, spiritually perfect state of being. You do not have to sit in lotus position saying a mantra or have a tranquil mind with no thoughts. Meditation is intentional, internal focus.

Many studies confirm the positive impact of meditation on physical health – it reduces stress, improves sleep, reduces physical pain, and improves cardiovascular function.

For empaths prone to depression meditation is an immediate tool to change our thoughts and clear energy.

Meditation, or just mindfully noticing your internal and external self, using the breath and quiet, shifts your thoughts away from a negative spiral or loop. It's an opportunity to hush the chattering "monkey mind" of repeating conversations, or events – to get off the path of worry. Getting distance from the mental noise allows glimmers of insight to solve problems bringing you down. Meditation naturally makes you feel better and opens the door to a calmer mind and improved mood. Even a shift from feeling heavy and gloomy to feeling neutral – neither good nor bad – is a welcome relief.

As a psychically sensitive person, it's the best way to notice and improve the quality of energy in your body and your energy field to change how you feel emotionally and physically. Meditation is a way of coming home to yourself with attention, breath, intention, and awareness.

The most straightforward and natural way to meditate and move energy is a powerful psychic tool called grounding. It is essential for sensitive people who attract and heal energy from people and places and feel and act as if it is their own. You can use grounding as your only meditation practice or use it first before starting another process.

In the Midwest where I grew up, houses have grounding rods to protect the electrical systems from being destroyed in the event lightning strikes a home. The grounding rod attracts and takes the hit, moving the excess energy into the Earth where it can be grounded out and safely distributed.

Your grounding rod is a connection to the Earth from the base of your spine. It can look or feel like anything to you – a rope, a tree, a rainbow, a simple line, a big pipe – whatever. This connection plugs you into the Earth to release unwanted energy and emotion to settle your energetic field and thus your entire nervous system, and help you feel safe, secure and relaxed. There are three necessary steps to this simple meditation: Ground, Release, Fill up. That's it. You can take 20 minutes to do this or one minute, ten times a day. Once you get a feel for grounding and releasing, it's easy to use at the moment as needed. Here's an abbreviated version of this meditation:

1. Sit comfortably with your eyes closed and take three slow, deep breaths.
2. Drop your attention down to the base of your spine. Settle in and feel the pressure of your tailbone touching your chair and let your awareness be right there.
3. Imagine a connection growing from the bottom of your spine deep into the Earth. It can look like anything: a tree root, a big pipe, a line of energy.
4. As you connect, any energy, thoughts, or feelings you want to release are pulled easily by gravity down out of your space. As you breathe you pull healing Earth energy back up through your feet and legs.
5. Allow the energy to release as you imagine a golden ball of energy above your head filled with your light and wisdom. Bring this down through your body to surround you in a "bubble" of you.

Over the years I've found that grounding is the single most effective tool to shift your experience quickly when you are having a rough time. You can even "ground" other people, places, and situations. I used it on my kids when they misbehaved in public, or on a line of cars in traffic to settle the chaos and move things along. Just attach a grounding connection to anyone or anything to make positive change. It's a modern-day version of a magic wand! For a more detailed version with step-by-step instructions see Appendix I.

A meditative or reflective practice, no matter how simple, is a must for out-of-control empaths and psychic sponges. Even if you think you don't see or feel the energy, intentional practices or routines clear your energy field and directly affect your physical health, like pain and illness, and the vibration of your feelings. The higher the vibration, the more positive the experience. The physiological benefit is real for skeptics and believers alike.

When you think about someone out of the blue or feel obsessive worry about another, like your kids, their energy is in your space. And more than likely your energy is in theirs where it does no good. It depletes you and interferes with them. Being mindful and meditating gives you the chance to notice and separate, allowing you and others their own path of experience.

For example, by taking the time to drop down out of my head and lower into my body each morning or as needed throughout the day, I experience a physical shift in my appearance and posture as I relax unnoticed tension from my muscles. A calm, soothing voice takes the place of a critical, worried one. My thoughts turn from solving other peoples' problems or making emergencies out of non-emergencies. From this calmer mind, I'm open to choosing the right action to take for the day – I get insight on where to focus my efforts, and my work or plans go smoothly. Taking confident action keeps my thoughts and mood up and keeps me on a positive, purposeful path. I start my day off with the best parts of me in the driver's seat and wind up getting where I want to go.

In a relaxed state of mind, breathing deeply, there's a better chance higher wisdom can settle in to assist us.

Getting our "feet on the ground" through meditation and rooting into our bodies is essential. It's through this connection that we find our own radicle root, like the first and longest center root of a tree that bursts from a seed. In grounding, we find our essence.

I never tire of watching the transformation as I talk clients through the process of grounding for the first time. At the start of a session, most are fidgety and strained. Indecision, anxiety, or worry disrupts the flow of energy in and around them and makes their aura look and feel jagged or weak. Or depression's heavy energy hides them so well it's impossible to see the light of their Soul. After grounding, their faces soften and flush with warmth. They are "behind their eyes," present and focused. Their arms relax and open as they sink deeper into the chair, and their energy feels solid, whole and approachable. Even those mired in pain and suffering at the start of the meditation feel a difference at the end. That difference is the light of separation from depression, or from others energy and emotions. It has revealed itself, and people feel better and with that feeling comes a moment of clarity. They understand now how to move on, what the answer or next step is for them. They see what they've misinterpreted or done wrong and feel compassion and possibility for themselves. There is hope. Something can change.

Be creative with your form of meditation. If a misconception about meditation keeps you from healing and growing this way, then release it and make up your own.

My client Teresa, a self-proclaimed Type A personality, who was also in the throes of profound grief from her husband's sudden death, found it impossible to focus and sit still. She adopted her morning routine of holding a hot mug of coffee and sitting with her dogs as her meditation.

Breathing in the steam and smell of the coffee took her into her body. The slow, repetitive movement of petting her dogs calmed her nerves and softened her tense muscles. She committed this time first thing to find quiet in herself as much as possible, setting the intention to feel calm for the rest of the day, instead of entertaining worried thoughts that kept her off her path.

There are endless ways to incorporate meditation into your daily routine. Perhaps you're a person who gets excellent answers and ideas in the shower – it's a comfortable, transformative space to use as your meditation practice. Just an extra five minutes to set the tone for your day with intention is empowering, and often magical.

Visualize washing away problems, concerns or unwanted energy of people, places, and things in whatever form you experience it. With closed eyes and deep, slow breaths, imagine it all going down the drain as if clearing yourself head to toe of mud and grime.

Then let the water wash over you, bringing in what you need. See a color that feels healing, or you can focus on your breath as you affirm a flow of light and support drenching you. See the water now connecting you to the earth as it flows down the drain. One stream of energy from heaven through you to the Earth.

Mindfulness throughout the day is enough to open the door to intense listening. Slow your physical actions and take in your surroundings; feel the warm water on your hands as you wash dishes or the soft cotton sheets as you make your bed. Inhale the scent of onion and garlic rising from the stove. Turn your natural ability to notice everything in a more positive direction that serves you by tuning into your surroundings, your breath, and your body. You get immediate feedback about how you feel, what you need for clarity or focus, and an awareness of what makes you happy.

Though technology is a significant source of our dis-connection, you can use it positively to reconnect using a multitude of free meditations on YouTube or use sites like Head Space and Insight Timer. Being guided through meditation or breathing to music is just as powerful as meditating by yourself and can take the pressure off of you to do it "right." These are great applications for teenagers to use too because it fits their lifestyle. They can fall asleep to it, calm test anxiety, or lift their mood using their phone.

My friend Kathryn Remati started meditating when she was 16 to learn to relax in response to the stress and heartbreak in her life. Now grown up, and an internation-ally known meditation teacher, she created an app to talk herself through the meditation she wanted to hear but couldn't find. She also wanted a way to quickly reach out and share the benefits of what she learned with others that made it easy and accessible. Her app includes guided meditations to ease or eliminate insomnia and promote self-love, two significant issues that contribute to depres-sion. You can find her beautiful words and music at www.tranquil-me.com.

How do you listen? Slow down. Breathe. Pay attention. Get to know yourself better by anchoring into your body and connecting to your inner life of thoughts, feelings, and energy.

You can't change what you don't know exists. The more you listen, the more you learn how to live a successful life with depression at your side. You never know what or who will show up to teach you.

Chapter 10

BANISHED PARTS

While it's clear thoughts create our emotional state, tuning in even more to feelings amplifies the thoughts to better hear what drives our actions. Every emotion has a voice, trying to get our attention.

No one likes feeling jealous, fearful or greedy. We despise feeling stupid, unworthy or ashamed. So, we learn to banish or suppress these so-called "negative" feelings from our emotional life to avoid pain or discomfort, to pretend we're strong, or to fit in.

Suppressed feelings and resulting behaviors have a link to traits we dislike about ourselves, or an emotional family legacy we are trying to hide. The problem is when we relegate one side of our self to the shadows we risk losing other desirable qualities too. Feelings are like people. They have personalities and purpose. As we meet our feelings inside, we understand their essential role in our wellness.

We need emotional complexity to enliven and push us off our accustomed flat-lined existence and create the natural balance of dark and light we unknowingly seek to feel fulfilled. Reclaiming voiceless parts of ourselves along with depression brings them out of the shadows of unconsciousness where they sabotage our success. Feelings like joy, enthusiasm, delight, and sensuality need a stage too because if not allowed expression they wind up in the shadows and take on new, less desirable forms. Often, we learned what feelings to hide as a child. Perhaps you were clingy or afraid at a critical point but got ridiculed and shunned for feeling fear. You grow up making sure not to show negative emotion, becoming a know-it-all who doesn't ask for help, or a bully who's not afraid of anything.

How often are we told we are "too much?" Too bois-terous, too sensitive, too nosy or too honest? So, we dial things down. We hold ourselves back and stop expressing ourselves, no matter what the feelings. When we do this, inspiration – which means "to be filled with Spirit" – dies. We must let our emotions talk.

Conversing with our shadows shows us more of who we are and opens the door to healing. When I stopped trying to get rid of my depression, I felt less depressed.

Why is that? Because of the universal law: what you resist, persists. Our emotional selves are invested in surviv-ing, including the part of us who wants to feel depressed, or at the least, is committed to the sad stories that keep us stuck. These parts demand center stage at different times in our life for a reason. They have a BIG message. It is up to us to stop and listen.

Give Depression a Name

It was one of those days when I was sick of being me – tired of being mired in the same hopeless place. On the outside, my life seemed beautiful. There was no real reason for me to be so down. But I'd been on a long stretch of feeling victimized by my usual depressed rant. It told me I'm so lame, other people just suck, life is shitty, and I have no reason to keep living. That familiar white noise of negative talk, like a TV in the background spouting lousy news, affecting my mood even though I'm not tuning into the details.

I sat frozen at my desk, unable to help myself. When I finally realized what thoughts were running in the background, I launched into self-pity. I'm going nowhere. How did I get so low again? Why can't I finish what I start and stop falling apart? Why do I keep falling in this hole?

I was asking the wrong questions. I didn't know what to do. The thought of asking for help didn't occur. Besides, who would understand?

At that moment, I decided if depression was here I might as well just let it take over. Why fight it anymore? I'm just going to give up and let this consume me. If I can't beat it, I'll join it. I looked straight on and addressed the roiling dark cloud enveloping me. That's when my relationship with depression changed. I gave it a proper name it deserved and addressed it out loud.[1]

"Hello, Depression, how are you?"

Desperate to meet Depression once and for all to understand why it always won out, I rose from my chair and opened the office door to let Depression enter and said, "Come on in. Have a seat right there."

I could see her in my mind's eye. She was a small girl in baggy clothes, with unkempt hair hiding her down-turned face. She felt dangerous, like dark boiling water beneath a heavy lid. The air in the room siphoned off to her, making it hard for me to breathe.

Her appearance and voice revealed how others see and experience me during my dark times. Looking at her let me see me. I asked her, "Where did you come from?" A fast-forward movie of memories flooded my mind.

Speaking aloud, I told her what I saw, acknowledging the pain of her past – what happened to her, what she felt, and why she wanted to be seen and heard. I reviewed everything that created the monster I wanted to kill.

Finally, as the memories ended, I asked, "What is your gift to me?"

She replied, "I help you see the dark in others. It's how you learned to heal. It's how you heal others."

Then came the question that restructured my thinking about Depression and me.

"What do you need to take a healthier place in my life?"

Her answers were fragments of words and pictures. "A hidden path. A dark place. A reminder of my wounds. A bowl placed for offerings. A way out."

Filled with compassion, understanding, and even appreciation, I saw her as an important, but separate part of me. Depression is not who I am; it's a place I go. And if it has a home inside of me, then I also want to give it a place outside me where I go with purpose and freely return at will.

Give Depression a Home

My conversation with Depression re-framed my identity as I realized I'm not condemned to being defined as a depressed person, clinically depressed, or "one who suffers from depression." I knew it intellectually but never seemed to accept it in my bones. Depression isn't all of ME. It is something I experience.

To separate myself but welcome Depression at the same time, I made it a real home outside me. My inspiration came through the work of Francis Weller, a psychotherapist specializing in grief and author of *The Wild Edge of*

Sorrow, who talks about the "banished" parts of ourselves that we grieve without even knowing it. These banished parts, like depression, and like the energy we resist but persists, need a home.

Giving Depression a physical space outside me allows me to visit it on the days it strikes. Honoring it with time and presence, and listening to what it needs, I can then leave and re-enter life, maybe not feeling joyful, but at least somewhere up the energetic vibrational scale that lets me move closer to peace.

Creating a home for Depression gives it a place in the world to reside, so it doesn't have to keep showing up and coloring every aspect of your life. It can stop stalking you. You've given it attention and listened. It has a place to be until the next conversation that inevitably arises because life and habits will inevitably call for it. But, cultivating a relationship with Depression builds trust. You know it can and will allow you space, and Depression knows you've not abandoned it and its needs.

Paradoxically, you must first go inside to meet and understand Depression to create a home for it outside yourself. Bring Depression out into the world, so you have space and distance from it to come and go as you please. Making a home for Depression can be a power-ful ritual, something profoundly personal that, as Weller notes, "elicits a certain vibration, a pitch, that enables us to individually or communally connect with the sacred."[2]

Ritual heals as it lets us step out of the ordinary into a place that remembers our inner rhythms – a sense of realness long forgotten. It is how we slip between worlds and unite the dark and the light. Engaging in ritual forces you deeper into yourself and connects with your Soul, opening the doors to your banished parts and your innate spiritual wisdom. You stop thinking and start feeling, allowing knowing. What you need bubbles up in ritual and greets you.

So, even if you don't feel compelled to invite Depression in for a conversation, try creating a physical home as lavish or simple as you like somewhere within your physical world.

Take a moment to ground. Tap into the deep pull of your sadness. Breathe deeply and ask: "Depression, where do you live?"

Be curious, as if you're asking about a new acquaintance. No need to strive for right answers. In what direction are you pulled? Do you get a fleeting image? Or hear a quick response? If not, no worries. Keep an open mind as you walk through your environment. Find a place in your home, garden, yard, or neighborhood and make it meaningful. It might be the corner of a dark closet, an abandoned alley, a forgotten and neglected spot in your yard.

Once you have a place, decorate Depression's home with the dark things that represent it – failures, griefs, disappointments. Use symbols of how being depressed feels, like massive stones, a dark cloak, or a rope that keeps you tied in place. Where does Depression feel most comfortable hanging out? That's the home you are making.

My Depression guided me to a far corner of our backyard that's partially hidden by a garden shed. A recent construction project made it an "out of sight out of mind" place with an unused compost bin, a rusted metal cage, fence boards, and cement. Dead pine needles blanketed the ground around two slowly dying pine trees we couldn't bring ourselves to cut down. It was a "dark" place energetically and one I'd been ignoring.

I chose the base of one of the pine trees as my place to sit and feel the weight of Depression, to contemplate death and dying when I face loss. It's nearly lifeless but still rooted and holds the wisdom of its years on this spot as it grew fifty feet tall. Here I considered the things in me that need to "die" – the people, beliefs, or behaviors I need to let go of to feel the way I want to feel.

Leaning against the tree, I felt its wisdom and loss, and know there is a gift inside Depression for me, as well. The deeper I know darkness, the more I can experience light. The roots underground in the dark let the tree grow to touch the heavens. So it is with me.

I prepared a new home for Depression, clearing out the junk and making useful what I could. As I worked raking needles, pulling weeds, and cutting bushes I held the intention of creating a new relationship with Depression. I stopped and talked to the pine tree and thanked it for its presence in my life – for the deep shade, and a trunk to hide behind as I sit at its roots to enter my personal underground. I gathered pieces of nature and arranged them as an offering and contemplated what physical things I could offer to symbolize Depression. What made her feel at home? Once I created the space, I engaged Depression again to find out more.

"What," I asked Depression, "are you trying to teach me right now? What do you need to have a healthy place in my life? What can I do to make you stay home instead of running amok through my life?" The answer came clearly.

"I need to be taken care of."

Exhaustion came over me as I tapped into what felt like years of trying to be good enough, do enough for others, and to outrun all my fears. Depression is a child trying to cope in an adult world. She does not understand what to do. No wonder Depression needs tending!

I pressed on to find more to find a next step for me to take. "What does it mean to be looked after? What do you need right now?"

I saw her happily eating an ice cream cone. She relished the taste and laughed as it melted down her fingers. She was in no hurry and had nothing to do. For a moment she was carefree enjoying a treat all her own – like any kid deserves to feel. Later that day, I took myself out for ice cream – sending a powerful message of acknowledgment deep inside me with a simple, loving gesture.

Give Depression Respect

Creating and entering Depression's world is a sacred act – and ritual lets us see the sacred in anything we give attention, awareness, and meaning. Stepping into this place of reverence and awe anchors us inside, helping us ride the storms of emotion and life when they come. You discover that all of you is deserving. Suddenly, you see the blessing in the curse. Where ever you step, you are standing on sacred ground.

It doesn't matter anymore what cut the road to Depression. I've walked it so often there is nothing new to learn from past details of blame and shame. It is a deeply cut groove in my mind and psyche that I stumble down effortlessly because it is so familiar.

But I acknowledge Depression's arrival from where I am, bringing it forward into the present by addressing its needs now. When I find myself at the crossroads of depression or lightness, I have room to move in a different direction unhampered by the past. I can make a choice to spend more months in the rut of despair or take a slight turn down a new path through simple acts. The choice is within my power because I am aware.

My soul – that embodied essence of me as Spirit that is this lifetime lights the way. There are lanterns along the road – sparklers and road signs – that show up in people and experiences if I pay attention.

Chapter 11

WELCOME ALL FEELINGS

There is no inviting only one feeling into the circle when so many other important ones exist. Depression is a melting pot of the emotions, tamping down and hiding nuances in a flat line of existence that doesn't allow for feeling anything. Once you see Depression for who it is, others are easier to spot as well as the essential supportive role they play. The home of Depression has rooms visited by these guests.

Grief

At the heart of what we call depression often lies grief, which comprises a crazy-making soup of conflicting feelings. There are the obvious things we grieve – like the death of a relationship or a loved one – that create depression even in those who've never experienced it before. The sadness of loss is immense and all-encompassing. It can't be discounted and requires special care when we are in the midst of it.

Nothing in our culture prepares us for grief after losing someone or gives us a place for it to dwell in a way that feels sustained and safe enough to see us through the bleakest days. You might believe (or are told) that you should grieve alone and not burden anyone with your feelings or should put up a good front and keep moving. People might disappear in the dark face of your sorrow or expect you to be done with it before you're ready. You might fear if you touch the center of that pain, you may never come back.

Ellen came to see me several months after her only child was tragically killed while traveling abroad. She moved in slow motion from the waiting room to my office, appearing exhausted and spent, and spoke in a low, monotone voice. Connecting to her constricted energy field was difficult as she disappeared into grief. Her body was there, but she was not. Ellen wanted to be with her child and saw no future for herself without her daughter in it. Life was pointless.

***

There is a spiritual energy that weaves humanity together. Within our closest circle of friends and family that web tightly wraps around us. It is our field of experience, our "normal," our life. When someone precious leaves this realm, that fabric wrenches apart, disrupting everything within our energetic field. The nervous system becomes overloaded – insomnia, fear, anxiety, and exhaustion take over. It is difficult to stay grounded in the present. We feel disembodied – with one foot in this world while the other seeks higher ground beyond the physical plane where we sense our loved one has gone.

Though it's no longer customary to dress all in black or wear a mourning band on our arm, we need a signal to others and ourselves that says, "I am not myself. The world is not the same. Please respect and excuse me while I grieve."

From an energy perspective, it is essential to rebuild the structure torn apart by grief, and that's best accomplished through self-care like rest, good food, nurturing by others.

Acknowledging the power of grief to undo us and reaching out to diminish its force by sharing with people who understand your pain helps carry you to a lighter place eventually. Grief needs a voice, and communal space to hold it when it is too much to bear. Ask and allow someone to take care of you. When you are strong and so inclined, take care of someone else and lift them up to mend the rift in your heart. For more extroverted people, channeling grief into action to make meaning of what was lost transforms them and others. Countless organizations and charities that educate, inspire, and support others were born out of grief.

In times of significant loss, listening to grief to give it what it needs, grounding your energy, and paying particular attention to your empathic sensitivities are essential to moving through to finding a new "normal." From there, it's possible to build a bridge back to meaning.

Even if you haven't suffered a loss through death, grief creates an undertow of sadness. What if our depression is a deep longing for things lost we never considered?

Like grief for the positive parts of ourselves that we banish as well – our enthusiasm, joy, curiosity, creativity – our child-like self that held the magic of hopes and dreams. The parts of us we diminished to fit in and be accepted.

We grieve little losses and big ones daily – everything from the dead bird on the side of the road, to the status of a job, or the green hills plowed under by more needless development. We grieve slippery things we can't pin down that make us nostalgic and wistful for the past. We feel an unrecognized sense of loss for safety and morality – a time we thought we knew what the rules were but now they've changed.

Grief is heavy like depression and sits in the dark too making us weepy or numb. They are kindred spirits, two faces of the same coin. Grief builds over time with us unaware, and, in the words of Francis Weller, it is this "growing weight of unattended sorrows" that often gets misdiagnosed as depression. Our heavy hearts are full of "congested grief." Is it any wonder, Weller asks, that the number one cause of death in our society is congestive heart failure?[1]

Noticing and naming Grief in all the ways it shows up transforms it. As with Depression, it needs an outlet to move from the dark into something else.

When a wave of grief comes, place one hand on your heart and with closed eyes, breathe deeply to let it move through you. Breathing in acknowledges its presence and importance, breathing out releases the energy and keeps it from settling like a stone on your chest.

Sharing is important to articulate the intensity of grief and loss but do so in a way that doesn't keep you mired in it. As an empath, it's critical to connect with people and experiences that acknowledge the pain of grief but give you support with positive action and reminders of hope and healing. Find a role model who lives life after the loss that inspires you. Grief counseling, grief groups through a church or city adult education programs or workshops employing ritual to process grief, are all potent ways to find the light in the dark.

If you grieve the loss of what was – whether it be your youth, an open meadow full of flowers, or a stimulating relationship – find ways to cultivate the feelings tied to what's missing to re-experience it in a new way. As we discuss later, re-discovering what has heart and meaning on a soulful level patches the places in us where life force ebbs away, giving us more to draw comfort from when we need it most.

Anger

We've all heard depression is "anger turned inward." I believe it, and I see it from an energetic perspective in others as a black hole, pulling in light from all parts of our life and consciousness. Anger is powerful, and that's why we fear it. It feels destructive and dangerous, so we spend an incredible amount of energy keeping it under control. It's like holding a beach ball underwater – it takes focus, strength, and commitment. We think we do a good job hiding our anger, but it pops up unexpectedly in our conversations and thoughts as sarcasm, criticism, or pas-sive-aggressiveness. We force anger down with destructive habits like over-eating or drinking. When it explodes, we appear awkward and off balance as we struggle to push it below the surface. Holding in anger is exhausting.

Anger and the enormous effort we spend controlling it locks up our creative power within it. It guards the door to our essence as it sits in the first and second chakras centered in our pelvis and gut and impacts emotions, sex-uality and survival. It is, as I saw once in a client, a "Dark Buddha," fierce and powerful. A master spiritual teacher so incredible that to acknowledge its presence might blow the world wide open. When you get a sense of its enormity, it feels if you get angry, say what you really mean and stop being a victim, you will die. (Or someone else will!).

I understand that this is the place once feeding my

suicidal thoughts. A see-saw between powerless and power – landing under the depressive weight of having no control and believing I can't save myself, nobody will rescue me, and no one wants me here, so maybe I should go. The destructive force of my anger and power turned in on me like a nuclear cell overheating and about to blow.

Use anger's constructive force to clear your energy and emotions by tapping into the fierce rage of your own Dark Buddha pooled deep in your bowels and pelvis. Squat low like a Sumo wrestler and yell from deep in your gut, sticking your tongue out, eyes bulging. Bear down with all your pelvic muscles and push on your bladder and bowels and birth or expel your anger. RELEASE. Then relax by coming up slowly, scooping Earth energy up as you stand and pull` it through your first chakra, your body, and out the top of your head. See a grounding connection to anchor and keep you steady. Fill up with creative, nurturing earth energy and thoughts and images of what you want to replace anger. Remember, nature abhors a vacuum. Once empty something comes in to takes its place so choose the quality of the energy and emotions you want there instead.

It feels odd to empty out to lose an old friend like anger or just the stagnant energy of others that surrounds it. Again, it's imperative to fill up, not with something to mask the emptiness like food, alcohol or sex, but a sense of presence – your own – in that space.

Disappointment

What does Disappointment feel like to you? For me it is physically crushing, like a massive, wet cloak thrown over my head, covering my body, making it impossible to breathe. My thoughts wail, saying I'll never have what I want – ever.

Bouncing back from disappointment is a skill – it's called resilience and more than anything, research is showing, it determines happiness. Some people are naturally good at it – you and I may not be, but that doesn't mean we can't be!

We experience various emotions every day on some level, and disappointment is no different. How do you learn to handle it? What can it teach you if you look back at past disappointments or those that weigh on you in the present?

I had two major disappointments in recent years back to back that ultimately pushed me to a better place. In 2012, my husband was offered a position to work in Germany for three years. It was a dream come true!!! We made our plans, started saying our goodbyes – and then the job opportunity fell through.

Deep in the funk of disappointment, I looked for what it could teach me. I realized how much I was expecting me to be different by moving, and forgot that "wherever you go, there you are." If I wasn't thrilled with myself, my home, my work, or my health here in California then moving wouldn't magically make it so. I was forced to look for all the qualities of the life I thought we could have had in Europe and bring them into the one I was living. Learning starts with questioning who or what shows up to teach us. How do I feel that my life is already a dream come true now?

Putting pen to paper got me through. I wrote all the "what if's" and "if only's" that cluttered my thinking and worked my way to answering those questions that eventually helped me shift. How do I find beauty and newness and feel more abundant? Where can I experience new cultures close to home? What will bring us closer to each other and to our community? How does my work fit into where I am now?

Getting precise about the life I want and steps to take in the present put everything in perspective. From that point, I focused on more creative time writing and growing my business differently. It became easier to let go of the things that didn't bring me joy – who needs a clean house at all times?

I then took on a health challenge. For years I'd lived with constant pain because of a worn-out knee. Walking more than a short distance was excruciating – stairs and hills were a nightmare. It was embarrassing! I felt old way before my time, and I held my family back from having fun.

I decided it was time to take responsibility for my health and demand surgery (doctors kept telling me I was too young and to wait as long as possible). I scheduled a total knee replacement for the fall and did all I could to get stronger and lose 15 pounds. I was upbeat and confident I would bounce back quickly and be pain-free.

I was so wrong. After a few days, the sciatic nerve running from my hip to my foot burned as if on fire. The pain increased when I tried to bend my new knee and strengthen my leg in physical therapy. I could only bend so far and could go no further. The back of my leg would tighten and freeze, and I couldn't breathe. After weeks of trying my knee became frozen from scar tissue. Not only did I have nerve pain, and a now stuck knee, I was one of the unlucky 5% of people whose leg doesn't wholly 'wake up' after surgery from the nerve block inserted to reduce pain. The inner side of my calf was numb.

For the next year, I chased answers and healing – new surgeons, physical therapy, acupuncture, massage, Rolfing, energy work, meditation, Pilates – trying to get more movement. Still, I couldn't get my knee to budge or the searing pain from my hip to my toe to go away. I was worse than before my surgery. Talk about disappointment!

The gift in this disappointment was being forced to slow down even more and listen to what my body had been trying to tell me long before the surgery. I looked deeper for answers and wrestled with the truth about long-held emotional and energetic pain now showing up as physical pain in my back and leg. I confronted being powerless, and how I avoid being power-full. I had to humbly ask for help over and over, and learn how to ask for it in the right places. I dove into my wisdom, trusting my intuition, and the mind-blowing truths that come to consciousness when you ask your body "show me what you need."

I still can't bend my knee as I should, but I'm stronger than I've ever been both emotionally and physically. I don't doubt I will continue to heal in ways that allow me movement and freedom. And I'll gain the strength to move forward with a power to live a happy life. It is a distinct metaphor, but those are the ones we overlook. The lessons in our life stories are there to read when we pull back far enough from emotions to see them!

Powerlessness

It took a long time for me to see that identifying with my past instead of the present committed me to play the victim and stay in pain. I now recognize this part of me as Weak, and she has her distinct kind of power – the power to suck people in, suck them dry, and drain the life force from me. Weak is another unsatisfied black hole. It's an aspect of me nobody else wants to be around.

Being raised by hardworking folks who grew up on farms and later became entrepreneurs instilled a sincere belief in self-reliance in me. My parents, especially my mother, were not complainers. Life is work, and if God is merciful, you can work until you die. As a result, I view asking for help as a sign of weakness and feeling weak or powerless as a bad thing. I try to kill off the feeling of Weakness. I get tough on myself and others, doing more, expecting more. I work harder, longer, faster.

In my rush to feel empowered, I discovered an unat-tractive tendency when I sometimes encounter people who appear "weak" (soft-spoken, a sullen face, droopy body posture, emit victim energy). I become extroverted and competitive and want to prove that I know more than them, or I'm strong enough to "take care of them." My confidence level rises to a place of arrogance – compassion goes out the window.

There is a part of me who wants to 'crush' the weakness right out of them and get it out of my sight, so I don't see and feel the weakness it's reflecting in me. But then I get caught up in a hidden belief that power is "bad," it means I'm some "bitch" who thinks she's better than others. I don't want to be one of those people. I can never win. I can't be powerless; I can't feel the power. Does this sound familiar to you too?

I see now there is this spectrum of Weak/Power-less--- Strong/powerful. There's good and bad on both sides. Good has "bad," bad has "good." When you get quiet and ask what is below the surface, when you invite everything in for an honest conversation, it is astounding what shows up.

Only when I talked to and accepted my Weakness, did I understand who she was and where she came from. As a small girl being molested by a man who had not only a physical advantage over me but also influence over my dad's job and our family security, I was powerless.

Utter helplessness feels like you will die. It's a horrible feeling I wanted to avoid at all costs – so any reminder of that powerlessness sent me right into being the aggressor. How do you get power when you're powerless? Go after someone weaker than you.

When I invite Powerless/Weak in for a conversation, she shows me her true colors. She is childlike, quiet and reflective; she notices beauty, is sensitive, and kind-hearted. The gift in her is that she tries to tell me I want to be taken care of and what it is I need to feel that way. She leads me to what Depression needs too.

And being taken care of is not a bad thing. We all need it. It is again our natural state to want to be nurtured – whether it's your kid taking out the trash every week without being asked or a caring friend bringing you soup when you're sick – there are hundreds of ways we can feel cared for looked after and loved.

As we welcome all feelings, we understand and listen to what we need. Not the false needs of drink, food, or shallow entertainment that soothe but don't cure, and in the end, hurt us. But the simple, at the moment kinds of things that meet our needs and change our moods. We're more flexible, satisfied, and far less stressed, inviting long forgotten friends like Joy, Patience, and Love back into our life.

Chapter 12

CARE OF THE SOUL

Jasmine nervously gathered her things as I met her in my waiting room. Dressed in pastel yoga clothes, she softly apologized for being late, though she wasn't. She gently shook my hand and gave me a sweet smile.

Once seated in my office, the sofa swallowed her petite frame, making her look much younger as she explained why she'd come to see me.

Since her mother's recent death, Jasmine felt a growing dissatisfaction with her life. Fear drove her to me for answers after developing an erratic heartbeat. "Can you see what was causing it?" she asked. I could, but it wasn't a real broken heart, but rather her "energetic" heart, the place that connects us to our Soul. Metaphorically, the heart holds our longings, and what we love.

We talked about what her heart might be trying to tell her, and the energy I saw there and in the rest of her aura, and how it was reflected in the way she lived. She told me she feels guilty taking time for herself and puts others' comfort and concern before her own, even family members she didn't like.

Some would call her a people-pleaser, who rarely says what she wants and acts on it. She'd spent years playing small to appease her mother, taking care of her mother's house and finances even though they had a rocky relationship.

Though retired, Jasmine's calendar is always full of errands and volunteer work. Her kids drop off the grandkids without warning, and she never says "no."

As we worked together over several months, she came to understand how over giving and neglecting her own needs, desires, and personal space was wearing down her heart, draining her life force, and her overall sense of self-worth. By the end of our sessions, as she acted to create time and space just for her, the heart problem disappeared.

***

When we ignore our Soul for too long, our body directly reflects the emotional and energetic pattern in play as a final wake-up call. When things become physical, the need for change becomes real. Depression is the teacher that redirects us toward our purpose. It is a red flag that tells us we're not listening to our Soul.

Talking to Depression reveals an endless desire to be "taken care of," but like Jasmine, by over-giving out of fear, habit, or through unconscious empathic healing, we lose sight of our own needs. We ignore the clues our Soul gives us all the time trying to win us back to a better life. We are uninspired and depressed and even physically ill because we're cut off from our Soul.

Your Soul expresses your Spirit this lifetime – the things that make you, you. It is "a quality or a dimension of experiencing life and ourselves"[1] that is unique.

The Soul is that aspect of ourselves that keeps us together when we're out of our body floating away unaware with our head in the clouds or get so tied up in the materialistic world we lose sight of our bigger spiritual self. The soul holds together "mind and body, ideas and life, spirituality and the world."[2]

We find and connect to soulful things energetically through the heart (or fourth) chakra, which symbolizes the parts of our consciousness concerned with our closest loving relationships and our perception of love and acceptance. It's the center of giving and receiving, including being able to love and give to ourselves.

When our Soul and our heart chakra are out of balance by overextending ourselves for others or ignoring our deepest needs, we feel floaty, ungrounded, and have no real sense of self. We fear being hurt because being untethered makes us unsure. We feel lonely. When the heart chakra is underactive, it's hard to feel joyful.

When a place or person is soul-less, there is no "there" there; no depth or breadth, no character or sense of authenticity. Losing touch with our Soul means living on the surface, robotically surviving without meaning or real interest in anything. A soul-less life is devoid of fun, passion, and connection, a genuine sense of self. It makes us sick.

I see this "soul-sickness" in clients experiencing depression, whether it has been lifelong, or situational due to recent events. Either they have never acknowledged the call of their Soul or have neglected it for years by giving up the things they love. The result is the same – the familiar feelings of emptiness and disillusionment with how their life, work, or relationships turned out. They yearn for personal fulfillment and meaning. They crave a soulful experience even if they don't realize that's what is missing. Life is our Soul challenging us to grow.

Soul sickness is a chronic condition like any other; without our health, nothing else matters. We must take responsibility for curing what ails our Soul by acknowledging how precious it is – like our empathic power – and give it the medicine it deserves.

Soul sickness prevails among women because we're natural nurturers, especially moms who have built their lives around caretaking, and it's hard to see how much we over-give. Becoming a mother is a crash course in self-sacrifice, as our world shifts from our needs to put the care of a little one front and center. Under the stress of being a new mom and afraid of messing up, we master anticipating their needs. Over time we become conditioned to put others first, never noticing the subtle undertone of fear that if you don't something terrible might happen. It's a hard habit to break and can leak out to taking care of adult friends, family, and co-workers who don't need (or want) it.

How much do we take care of others without realizing we're doing it? Do we know when to draw the line with our children and let them take care of their own needs to become healthy, capable adults?

Caring for your Soul is at the heart of living unrestricted by depression both literally and figuratively and what feeds the Soul are those things close to our heart. What has heart and meaning to you? What makes your heart sing? What do you love? If you don't know, think back – what did you love to do when you were five years old?

Consider the people who you admire and respect. They often reflect your qualities indicative of your Soul. What places, cultures or languages draw you capture your imagination? The "I've always wanted to…" things you dream about. These are clues to the environments, behaviors, and experiences of a soulful life.

Recall times when you felt deeply relaxed and restored. What were you doing? What was the quality of your surroundings? How do you like to recharge after a long week? When you make time that's good for the Soul; whether it's hanging out with your dog or rowing a kayak across a lake, you strengthen the connection to your higher spiritual self.

We take care of our Soul when we commit to what's important by scheduling time, sustaining new rituals and activities, and allowing ourselves to enjoy life. Soulful things become the essential small things we can take credit for doing well. Every time we act to feed our Soul we affirm our worth.

A New Kind of Soul Food

How we "feed" our Soul through our body is important on a practical level too.

To numb our pain or lift our spirits we often medicate our soul-sickness with food – it's an easy and accessible drug that often hurts more than it helps by creating a web of avoidable health issues. For me, getting sober and quitting smoking was far easier than giving up sugar. I joke that sugar is my "heroin," but it's not an exaggeration. A 2009 study showed that sugar is eight times as addictive as cocaine while other studies confirm it and other so-called healthy artificial sweeteners are more addictive than heroin. I still struggle back and forth with sugar because it is everywhere. Once it gets in my system, it's hard to kick it again. There are over 600,000 processed foods in the US, and over 80% of them contain sugar.

Much is in the form of high fructose corn syrup, which is outlawed in other countries.[3]

The food industry has mastered engineering food to purposely create an addiction to their products, just as the tobacco industry did with cigarettes. Sugar lights up the pleasure center of the brain and releases dopamine; the "feel good" chemical critical for a healthy emotional life. Used in excess, sugar and processed foods decrease dopamine receptors, meaning it takes more sugar to feel good. We're fighting not only food chemical warfare to maintain our moods, but our instinct toward pleasure in the brain, and our programmed need to eat for survival.

Knowing we're up against powerful chemical and physical reactions by becoming educated about what's really in our food takes the guilt out of abusing food. It makes it easier to choose what's healthy when you see the truth. Information about how to eat better is everywhere, but it's overwhelming and confusing. I've found the best first step is to start with as much "real" food as you can. No boxes, bags or cans. Lean meat, fresh fruits and vegetables, and limited grains. And consider removing wheat from your diet and here's why.

Jessica watched her teenage daughter Katie go from a happy, healthy girl to a depressed, chronically ill mess in four years. Her symptoms varied from week to week; migraines, exhaustion, insomnia, nausea, body aches, congestion, chills, hot flashes, anxiety. Katie caught every cold and flu that went around school. Despite many doctors, tests, medicine, and supplements, the answer to her problem came down to this: food.

When Katie started eating "clean" – her symptoms diminished. Her energy and vitality came back, and she looked and felt truly happy for the first time in years. Not only was sugar wreaking havoc on her hormones and gut health, but she discovered an extreme sensitivity to gluten that never showed up in any bloodwork. Incessant nausea and frequent "flu" she'd suffered was caused by continuous poisoning from gluten.

Thoughtfully eating fresh, healthy foods feeds our soul in ways we can't overlook. And what we eat affects us far more than we realize, including our emotions. For years, we've understood that the mind impacts the body, but a new way of thinking based on studies in the last 15 years proves just how powerfully the body impacts the mind.

It's a relief to take the guilt and shame out of using food to avoid ourselves, and instead be able to have a healthy, enjoyable relationship with food. I've found the work of Dr. Mark Hyman, author of *The Blood Sugar Solution*, easy to understand and follow. Or consider finding a certified nutrition consultant locally like my friend Laura Halpin who empowers others to eat well by combining the science and spirit of nutrition in her work. (www.laurahalpin.com) Slowing down, being conscious, making food beautiful and nutritious feeds us on all levels by feeding our Soul.

A Soul-full life

When the heart chakra is in balance, we can give and receive love easily. We feel grounded and free to move between the spiritual and physical parts of ourselves. Ideas manifest here at the center where the upper and lower chakras meet, opening our experience of heaven on earth. We bring heaven down to earth by walking a spiritual path with grounded feet.

Soulful acts require imagination, reverence and a

willingness to enter both the dark and the light places and see the good in all. Taking care of our Soul is a sacred act that puts us in the center of the temple of our being with respect and devotion as an offering that sustains life – our life.

As we care for our soul, we become more refined. We choose and act based on our higher potential and desire, which brings us closer to living our purpose, no matter how simple or complicated. We live out our destiny with eyes wide open.

When we live a life full of Soul, it appears as Paulo Coelho says in *The Alchemist*, that "…when you want something, all the universe conspires in helping you achieve it."[4] A quietly extraordinary life of magical little miracles and synchronicity, rich with emotional experiences unfolds. Happiness on your terms delivered up in unimaginable ways.

My friend Hanna was overworked and overwhelmed starting up her consulting business. Feeling stressed about money and physically depleted made it even harder to help her clients and expand her services. Though fear told her to keep pushing and work harder, her body said otherwise, so she stopped to consider why making money always felt difficult and how or what she could change.

She canceled appointments for one day and sat meditating and writing about her relationship with money. She gardened and thought about how to let relationships and opportunity grow and still have time to spend with family and her flowers. She went for a massage and got the help she needed to relax her weary body. We talked at the end of the day, and she was clear on how she could reschedule work hours for more balance, feeling a renewed trust that money comes to her if she takes care of herself. We joked about contradicting the old saying "money doesn't grow on trees" and creating what she needs as easily as that.

The next evening, her aunt and uncle visited from out of town to celebrate her birthday. They walked in carrying a potted plant with money tied to the branches and coins buried in the soil. Her relatives were surprised by her tears and laughter as they unknowingly delivered a beautiful message from the Universe. A gift in the language of the Soul.

Willingness to take care of our self at this deep level brings us closer to Spirit through intuition.

Intuition guides us to what the Soul needs. The more we respond, the more our intuition and psychic sensitivity are validated and increased. As a result, we learn to trust to do what's right for us.

Chapter 13

INTUITION AND SPIRIT

When I feel anxious or worried, overwhelmed with deadlines and family demands, out of habit I work faster to complete through sheer physical will and by ignoring my feelings. Or, I procrastinate and avoid tasks I need to finish. When I get to either state I know I've come unplugged from the source of what saves me — the stream of higher consciousness that expresses itself through intuitive wisdom.

Intuition is the conduit between Spirit, Soul and the body. It helps us create heaven on earth.

When life feels hard, and I'm sucked into fear and sadness, I know immediately that I am cut off from intuition.

We fall into depression when we cut ourselves off from our Spirit, our Soul, and our body, so rediscovering intuition and how it "speaks" to us leads the way through the darkness. When I'm trying to find my way back to a lighter, happier place I start by actively seeking my intuition. I do anything to get back to the source of my power. I seek wisdom by getting quiet and asking the right questions to take me out of problems and align with solutions.

When we're connected to our Soul and caring for it, it speaks to us in the intuitive language of Spirit. We get insight and direction and don't feel alone. We feel empowered and less like a victim.

What is intuition? It's often called an inner voice, but it's much more than that. Because it is the link between the spiritual and the physical it takes on both other-worldly and worldly guises. It's the chills up your spine, the hair raising on the back of your neck. It's a book falling off the shelf when you walk down the aisle of the library in search of help. It's a feather at your feet, a tug in your gut. A sudden insight or scent of a dead loved one's perfume.

Intuitive guidance may appear as a mental image, a quick clear voice in your mind. It's a sudden uneasy or calm feeling, a broad sense of "I know it," or a healthy craving for a specific food or a place to visit to make you feel better.

It always has our best interest at heart. It doesn't leave us; we turn away in doubt because we don't trust. Once you're awake to your sensitivity as an energy being, you can more easily access your intuition and act on it consistently to live an authentic life.

Intuition is magical and practical. It helps you act like a grown up and make decisions. To act instead of hoping issues solve themselves.

When you think about it, life is all about making choices. In every moment we face decisions about how to be, what to do, how to feel. Most stress comes down to daily choices confronting us, and if you have to make them alone with no partner, support or input, the pressure is even greater. Questions like "should I take this job," "what contractor should I hire," or "what's best for my children right now," keep us spinning in our minds with no resolution. Intuition cuts through indecision. At any point, on any matter, you can ask "what's the best action?" By aligning with inner guidance, you stop indecision and worry and act more confidently.

Following intuition grants access to your center of personal power, a place free of worrying about what other people think. With this inner source of wisdom, you're no longer dependent upon advice, affirmation or approval from others. You live more authentically, free of helplessness, and emptiness. You stop feeling like a victim when you choose a course of action instead of letting things happen. Intuition leads you from being quietly numb into a quietly extraordinary life. Life happens through you, not to you.

Intuition is knowing without knowing how you know. It appears when the logical mind steps out of the way, and information not readily or obviously available using the senses comes through. It is direct, immediate, clear, and confident.

For instance, we needed to buy another car for our daughters but couldn't find what we wanted. What could have been a fun search turned into another chore we had to do "right" and get done. After three months of looking and indecision, I realized we were making the process too hard.

I sat outside to meditate and reflect on how easy it is to create what we need when I tap into intuition and let it guide me. I envisioned how much fun I had finding Phillip's car several years earlier when I spotted it at a car dealer while out on an errand and heard a voice say "there's Phillip's car." It was a beautiful blue convertible with low miles and an incredible deal. As I settled into the energy and feelings of that experience I imagined finding our next car as easy and placed an order with my inner wisdom, "I want a black Audi A4 in good condition with low mileage for $16K."

I smiled to myself, confident that what we needed would show up.

While watching a basketball game with my husband the next evening, my attention zeroed in on an Autotrader commercial. I had the thought "Look on Autotrader," so I jumped up and got my laptop. I typed in the make and model and the first car to pop up was a black Audi A4 with 48,000 miles available at a car dealership four miles from our home for $16,742. I turned the screen toward Phillip and said, "Here's our car!"

The next day Zoe and I went for a test drive. The car was perfect. I checked in with myself to see if this was the right time to buy and felt calm. It felt easy. The "cherry on top" from the Universe appeared when I scanned the sales contract and saw our new car's manufacture date – 3/3/2012 – the same birth month and day as my daughter.

Tapping into Intuition

Tapping into intuition uses the same techniques as listening to your thoughts and feelings. Slow down and cultivate quiet reflection. Breathe. Take your logical mind "out of gear" to let intuition come through. The more you get to know and distinguish between the banished parts that sabotage you, the easier it is to hear your intuitive guidance.

When considering an issue or goal, ask the right questions of your inner teacher to open up to wisdom. Don't ask "why" but rather "what" or "how." Start by asking straightforward yes and no questions to keep from complicating issues.

When you get an answer, sit with it and notice internal clues. How do you react emotionally? How do you feel physically? Remember intuition goes toward truth and growth. Your answer might scare you, but it also makes you feel alive.

When you ask intuition for help, it responds with guidance and answers. But, you must act on the information, or the connection shuts down again. You know how you feel when you give someone good advice, but they refuse to take it? Don't do that to your intuition!

Remember the power of small actions to accomplish big dreams or to answer big questions. What can you do today to act on the intuitive guidance within that helps you feel how you want to feel and moves you toward happiness?

Be patient and notice. Intuition isn't always immediate and is not always what you expect. Don't be discouraged if when meditating or asking for guidance answers don't pop to mind right away. Stay open and aware to catch the diverse and creative ways intuition shows up. For example, you talk to a friend who mentions a book related to your issue; then you see a review in the paper. Hours later a stranger in the check-out line mentions the topic out of the blue. That's intuition throwing out the answer and shining a light on it to make sure you see it, confirming what you need.

Intuition wafts up from unconsciousness in our daydreams and night dreams. If you feel you don't connect in other ways, look there first. Don't ignore what's trying to speak to you. Spend time with your dreams, reviewing them with closed eyes before you get up. Write them down and study the messages.

Trusting Intuition

So how do you trust your intuition and know you're following the right direction? It can take time to learn how to hear it correctly. Like any skill, it takes trial and error, but the internal and external feedback you get points the way. If life gets more comfortable, problems resolve, and you're happier it's obvious intuition is working.

You'll experience a pattern of being inspired, acting, finding answers and then becoming more confident as you move through life.

It's easy to get thrown when problems show up despite your best efforts to do what you think is right. You choose, and things start to unravel. Now what? While it can be a sign you are off track, it doesn't mean you have to give up. Just check back in and keep fine tuning by asking, being open and aware, and acting as inspiration arrives. Look for sabotage. Are you listening to others or those so-called negative thoughts? Even the happiest and most successful people fail, so make friends with failure. Often it opens you up to learn substantially more in a faster way that propels you toward your desires.

There's usually a pattern to problems too. If you mentally trace them back, you can find where and when you didn't listen to yourself. Everything in the external world reflects our internal world. That's what intuition is trying to show you.

But sometimes challenges arise even when you're on track. As you shift and change old thought and emotional patterns and consequently how you behave, the quality of your energy vibration changes with you. Situations once acceptable to you no longer work. People you used to hang out with don't interest you anymore. It's not uncommon to lose people, leave places, and give up things as intuition aligns you with greater potential and away from what doesn't match an authentic life.

The framework of your life breaks down to build a foundation for new things to come. But the breakdown is a good thing – lost jobs, lost loves mean change is on the way. Some part of you knows this crisis is ultimately for the better when you honestly ask yourself. Like a woman who struggles after divorcing her abusive husband – even though it's hard there's still a clear knowing it was the right thing to do to live a better life.

Don't get scared off by what intuition hands you. Just because you know it is for your good doesn't mean you'll always be fearless. There is often risk involved, and that requires faith and trust. You step off the cliff, and the bridge appears. You reach for the breadcrumb, and the next one shows up to lead you further down the path.

Sudden success and opportunity brought on by following your intuition, and the surge of creative energy moving through you can feel overwhelming as you get accustomed to opening up to it. It can feel manic if you're not used to the level of energy, so using your grounding tool is a must.

At times Spirit moves faster than form toward fulfilling our purpose, and the body needs time to catch up. When success comes quickly, a too good to be true opportunity arises or a lofty idea pushes on you, that's when it's easy for the inner critic to say, "That's crazy, there's no way I can do that!"

A client who recently went through an unhealthy relationship and struggled to find a new home fell into despair. As she contemplated suicide and fell into a fitful sleep, she was shaken awake by a vivid dream showing her she couldn't die because her exquisite collection of healing stones first had to go to the Dalai Lama to aid in healing the world. Her vision was intensely real and left her feeling she needed to follow it through immediately.

Though she felt an urgent intuition, there are times we need the logical mind to step in and temper us. My client couldn't sell everything and run off to India to deliver her stones to the Dalai Lama, but she could look deeper into the meaning of that dream and see what she can do now to use her gifts in tandem with her stones to promote healing. Instead of throwing her life overboard in every way, she asked herself, "How can I continue to live in the world as a white, western woman in a way that feels in tune with the person I am?" That is the wisdom to follow in the moment that leads to understanding the bigger vision intuitive guidance offers.

Check your thoughts and if you doubt yourself or find problems persist, really listen. What are you telling yourself? Instead of saying "I'm so stressed. I'll never get this done," shift your tone and say something encouraging or comforting like "I'm doing well. I know this will pass and I'll feel better."

As your intuitive muscle gets stronger, you'll find it easier to go inside, shift awareness, ask for help and get answers quickly. For me, it feels like taking a step up and back in my consciousness into another space and time to pull in the information I need. It's a physical sense of being plugged in and feels like a bigger, wiser part of me is in charge.

Even when I did not understand intuition years ago, it still served me. It is this sense of something greater than me that has kept me alive for years. When I didn't feel like going on anymore, there was something, a voice I equate as my spiritual self, that would win out over the clamoring crowd in my head calling for blood and say "No, you don't get to die today. It is not your day."

It made me furious. Just let me out of this pain!! But I could never act on it. That calm, reasonable "true" voice came through loud and clear, stopped me in my tracks to rage and cry my way through, and sent me down a new path to try again. How often has intuition saved you?

Intuition gives us glimpses of our Spiritual self. Our Spirit is timeless, transcendent. It is the "you" I see with my eyes closed in a client session – pure energy, all-knowing, connected to all points of time and all things. We are Spirit having a physical experience, not the other way around. By going into the body, you find you are so much more than that. This is the breakthrough to self-realization. Each of us is a unique expression of energy, and like a thread weaving through a universal tapestry of energy, we join with others to create a design of patterns we call a lifetime. The thread continues to weave another design with both same and different threads to form the next life, expressing what's come before in a new and hopefully positive way as we spiritually learn and grow.

We move our Soul forward in purpose through the lessons of our experience, and the way we remember to do that is by rediscovering and trusting our intuition. It's how we live a spiritual life.

Spirituality is at the heart of resiliency and living a happier life and is a trait that you can embrace and cultivate. By connecting to this other, more significant part of yourself, you understand a connection to something even greater than you in this one life.

That power greater than us all is consciousness, "an

energy field created by all living things. It surrounds us, it penetrates us, it binds the galaxy together."[1] By understanding the force that moves within us and all things, we are better able to express what we came here for this lifetime and answer the question "what is my purpose?" By practicing spirituality, we bring "a sense of perspective, meaning, and purpose to our lives."[2]

I see this web of energy, I feel it. And I believe everyone sees and feels it too. It is us as Spirit, the sense of "heaven" within. We tap into that connection and each other through the higher vibrations of love and compassion. These are the doors that open our ability to see and know the truth.

Please understand that spirituality has nothing to do with believing in God or religion. I first heard about a "power greater than myself" in Alcoholics Anonymous. I hated it. By then I was also a "recovering Catholic," who wanted nothing to do with religion. Luckily, I met Sister Janet early in sobriety, a Catholic nun who told me to "fire that God and get a new one."

I clung to her advice to stay sober by seeking that mysterious force I suspected was real but couldn't name as a child. I felt "something greater" than me the day I got sober when I had what I later came to understand was a spiritual awakening.

I called in sick that Monday, too hung over and filled with self-loathing from drinking all weekend to show up at the office. But sitting at home depressed and wired with anxiety was painful so I walked to a grove of eucalyptus trees in a nearby park, alone on the path to a bridge in the center of the trees. Early morning fog encircled me, snaking through the trunks and branches of the grove.

It was beautiful and haunting. I stood shivering on the

bridge, wishing it was taller so I could leap from trouble for good. I hung my head, pleading with whatever was listening to help me because I couldn't help myself. I'm tired; I am done.

Within seconds, rays of sunlight shot through the fog in front of me. Relief poured into my body and fear left me. I suddenly understood that I could change direction in my life now if I wanted to. Peace surrounded me with the truth that no matter what, I would be okay. I made my way home, called a rehabilitation hospital and went in to talk to someone about my drinking. Despite the staff's protest, I left that day but promised to come back. I checked myself in a week later and never drank again.

You know you are living intuitively when you feel alive – flowing with life instead of pushing against it. You have more fun as life clicks with synchronicity and positive outcomes and you step in and out of remembering wholeness with ease.

Cultivating an intuitive life means you tap into your Spirit, into the universal energy of consciousness whenever you can, until you find your awareness there more than in the chaos of your mind or what's right in front of you. It's a soft remembering, over and over. *Oh yes, there's this.* Your life hums with this backdrop of wholeness. Even at the most painful, despairing times you can lift above or away and sense your Spirit – the purpose, the bigger picture. You detach and feel peace; you trust that the answers will come. No matter how bad you feel, a voice speaks up saying "I'm fine. All is well." It's the voice of faith.

Chapter 14

RE-CONNECTING

The quickest way back to our Soul and our Selves is through Nature. We are disconnected from our Souls because we're cut off from Nature in our daily lives.

For most of human history, we've lived in tune with, and at the mercy of our natural environment. We are humans, yes, but at our core, we are animals first, and we have that animal nature buried somewhere deep inside of us. There is a "wildness" in us that no longer gets met or expressed that needs to be close to the land, free, and moving and able to witness the brutality of life and death. To see extreme beauty in the sky, in creatures, and in the architecture of the landscape sculpted by wind, water, and fire.

We miss the kinship with animals as fellow beings and the pulse of life in plants. Sensing vague loss, we seek to fill that longing with other, needless things.

When do we get to feel the wildness in us? When do we ever get to be 'in the wild' and see life, exquisite, violent, unpredictable, yet perfect, as it is? The opportunity diminishes each year as we raze the planet in the name of progress and profit. Instead, we surround ourselves with concrete and stare at screens depicting "life."

Perhaps this is why we are fascinated with reality TV shows like *Survivor* or *Naked and Afraid.* We live vicariously through the suffering and the scintillation of being close to the edge with Nature, at the extreme of our physical self, hoping to feel more alive. It's why we obsess over pets and puppy videos online; why talking animals in movies and books draw us in. Our relationships with domestic animals reaffirm our long-forgotten tie to the wild. We seek the spiritual connections between humans and animals that have been a part of our experience for millennia.

When entering the fabric of Nature, we unite with omniscient wisdom that speaks to us of our past and our future. The door opens to intuition to come through with warnings and validation. Nature is a messenger of our Soul. It speaks to us in new ways when we've forgotten all other ways to listen. At some of my worst times, encouragement and answers have shown up in the form of an animal while I'm walking. Its presence is sudden, sometimes bizarre, but distinctly symbolizes what I need to know.

The first time I saw a bear in the wild, it came charging up an embankment next to me and ran in front of my friend Karen's SUV as we drove down a blacktop road near Mt. Shasta at midday. No time to react, we hit the bear but kept moving as Karen tried to stop. I glanced in the side mirror after the impact in time to see the cinnamon brown bear running behind us toward the woods on the left, dragging a broken leg.

Even before seeing the bear, it had been a weird morning. We set the alarm to wake early to go hiking but kept falling back asleep. Once on our way, we drove up and down the same road, unable to find the trailhead though it was clearly marked on a map. And later after hitting the bear, we found the trailhead but repeatedly lost our way, taking almost two hours to make the 45-minute climb to the small, glassy blue body of water held in a bowl of granite called Heart Lake.

Clearly, something was up. The Universe was speaking to us through nature, and as we later reflected long into the night about what it might mean, we knew only that we'd collided with what to us symbolized unconsciousness. Why couldn't we wake up? What do we need to wake up to?

Early on Monday morning after returning from our weekend trip, I woke to a call from Karen.

"I know why we hit the bear. Turn on your television," Karen said without a hello. Her tone made me run for the living room. I turned on the TV and watched the first of the World Trade Center towers collapse. I was awake.

Like the world that day, we awakened from a deep sleep of unconsciousness to realize the depth and reach of hate. We woke up to the sins of the past coming to haunt us at home. We woke out of naivete and entered a new world fraught with danger. Since September 11, 2001, the world hasn't slept in the same way.

Fifteen years later I saw a bear in the wild again. I drove slowly on Kanuga Lake Road near Hendersonville, North Carolina in the early evening looking for the last turn of my journey to Kanuga Camp. I came around a gentle curve and met a black bear crossing from the left. It stopped. I stopped. It calmly stood and looked at me as I fumbled for my phone without turning away from the beautiful creature in front of me. Our eyes met, then it loped from the center line in front of my car and ran down an incline toward the trees on my right. It put one paw on the top wire of a fence and leaped over gracefully.

I laughed and called out the window, "I guess you've done that a few times."

It seemed to hear me as the bear stopped and turned back to look at me. It paused as if giving me a parting message. I watched in awed silence. Fear rose for an instant in me as I thought of my first bear encounter. Is this a sign of something awful to come? Just as quickly, my inner voice responded. This bear is calling me from a different place.

The following week, millions felt another traumatic loss, but this time rising from the shadows within our country when Donald Trump was handed the presidency.

***

The perfection and beauty of Nature move me to tears. Color bursting from a field of wildflowers, the delicate symmetry of a spider web back-lit in the morning light, the thoughtful caretaking of elephants who stay behind with a sick or wounded family member. Nature's brilliance is all around us, in the way animals and plants interact to support each other or adapt to survive each other. It's in us too in the intricate and complicated workings of our bodies we take for granted and never, ever question. How we breathe, move, digest, fight off disease, process light, sound, and movement – all without thinking about it. We are amazing.

Nature is the place that brings us home to Self faster than anything. The disconnect and depression I see in clients ties to an unsatisfied spiritual connection to Nature that is not being met. It is their nature that's not satisfied.

And science proves what many have already felt all along. When we connect with Nature, we feel better.

In his book, *Blue Mind*[1], California Academy of Sciences researcher Wallace J. Nichols explores this shared belief in the essential need for nature by compiling research from fields like neuroscience and psychology that proves Nature, and especially water makes us not only happier but healthier.

These are a few highlights from the many research findings detailed in his book:

- In 2009, researchers from the University of Southern Maine studied veterans suffering from post-traumatic stress on a four-day Rivers of Recovery trip, one of many types of organizations engaged in ecotherapy, which recognizes the inherent healing capacity of nature. They found that among the veteran's depression lessened by 44 percent. Feelings of serenity increased 67 percent, assuredness by 33 percent, and positive mood went up 47 percent.

- Over 1.1 million responses to a smartphone app called Mappiness created to track subjective well-being showed we are happier outdoors in nature more than an urban environment. Even more so when people where near water.

- Autistic children who suffer from sensory overload and rarely smile or engage others socially transform with surfing or paddleboard lessons. According to program director Don Ryan of Surfers for Autism, "once they are on the beach you can't tell a kid with autism from any other child."

Other studies note that what makes people happy is being immersed in the senses – color, the sounds of wind, birds, and water, and the smells of flowers, earth, and ocean. To me, this confirms an essential connection to the body. If you're noticing your senses, you are coming closer to your SELF. Presence equals awareness of your spiritual nature reunited with Nature.

It's not just the animalistic nature embedded in our DNA that ties us to the Earth, but an energetic relationship as well. The Earth, like us, emits an electromagnetic field. It has an aura too, and we live in it!

I've talked about the advantage of grounding in meditation by visualizing a connection to the center of the earth using imagination to create the energetic awareness of being "plugged in." There is another powerful kind of grounding requiring a direct physical connection to exposed land referred to as "earthing" which underscores our need for Nature and further proves its healing power.

The universal rule of energy conservation states that energy is neither created nor destroyed; it is transformed, so we are all swimming in the Earth's "aura" and impacted by its movements. It takes no stretch of the imagination to consider that the more we resonate with the predominate creative life force of the Earth, the better off we'll be.

Earth energy naturally draws that which is out of balance to it and sends balancing energy in return. However, modern life cuts us off from the Earth's subtle energy because we spend our days in shoes, on concrete, and in the raised foundations of our homes and workplaces. We've lost touch with the source of vitality and aliveness emanating from the Earth, and this contributes to poor health.

Physical pain and illness, and sometimes medications taken to treat them contribute to depression, so eliminating chronic pain is critical to improving mood. Earthing is an active, empowered approach to healing, and best of all, it's free.

In the movie *Grounded*[2], nature photographer and filmmaker Steve Kroschel documents the power of earthing in great detail.

He tells how, after hearing about the concept of earthing, he tried it out of desperation to heal back pain and numbness caused by his intensely physical work running a center for orphaned wildlife in Alaska. Despite the deep snow, he managed to crawl under his house, strip down and lay naked under blankets on the exposed ground. Within minutes he calmed and relax. The next day his back didn't ache, and his hands weren't numb.

The movie covers his mission to spread the word of healing in his small hometown. With support from the man who discovered and researched the earthing concept, Clint Ober, almost 1,700 residents soon hooked into the earth with rods or with mats and connections plugged into the grounded electrical systems of their homes with astounding results.

To find out more about earthing view, the internet-friendly short film entitled *Prescription is Earth*.[3]

Nature wants us to thrive, just as we want it to succeed (or at least we should!). Lifeforce energy is reciprocal. When you give Nature the respect of your attention and care, it opens your energy field to receive healing on many levels.

As you tune into Nature and your nature, you see how the larger cycles at work influence your well-being. There's a reason humanity since ancient times has tracked the stars, has planted and harvested by the moon as it transforms from dark to light. Why rituals and holidays mark the seasons. We are along for the ride in the cycle of things whether we believe it or not. As the Earth goes, so do we.

Recognizing that a union with non-human life impacts our emotional experience opens the possibility to accept and prepare for reality. These are not forces to feel victimized by, but rather something to embrace, and through awareness, we use the energy of cyclical shifts to our advantage, or to at least consider when planning daily life.

Notice yourself within nature's larger world. Do you feel more motivated, less depressed and hopeful in the spring? Does your body ache as weather fronts move across the landscape toward your home? Does your insomnia happen near the full moon? Notice what weather or time of day makes you feel strong and use the time to your advantage and push ahead. When you feel out of sorts during the transit of certain seasons or planets, take time to rest and reflect.

This interplay with Nature often shows itself in tangible ways. For example, my mother and siblings suffer from what they call "the family curse" of sleeplessness for the two or three days when the moon is fullest.

As a new mother, I felt a mild panic rise in me in September as the sunlight and shadows shifted. Even though California weather is deceptively warm in the fall, I would dread the coming winter. I feared shorter days filled with low gray clouds that settled on me and dampened my mood. As a stay at home mom, it was hell being trapped inside with rambunctious little ones. I cycled further into depression during the winter, never realizing weather exacerbated it, and not some failure on my part.

Eventually, I read about Seasonal Affect Disorder (SAD) – a condition that's related to changes in seasons that begins and ends at about the same time every year. Symptoms start in the fall and continue into the winter months when diminishing sunlight can throw our biological clock out of whack and reduce levels of serotonin (a brain chemical that regulates your mood) and melatonin (a chemical which regulates sleep and mood).

SAD also has its specific symptoms that aren't always present with depression, such as heaviness in the arms and legs, frequent oversleeping, cravings for carbohydrates and weight gain, and relationship problems.

Doesn't this sound like our animal nature just doing what it needs? Like a bear going into hibernation, we're called to the cave of ourselves to wait out the winter. Life doesn't allow it anymore, but you can honor the need to go in with rest and meditation.

Knowing what I know now, I stay attentive to my mood as the season changes and do little things to help myself. I buy colorful fresh flowers and keep shades open and lights on to brighten the house. I take Vitamin D (naturally produced by sunlight in our body) to ward off achiness in my muscles. I look for the beauty in winter instead of focusing on lifelessness.

Fortunately, we can replicate sunlight through exposure to specialized full spectrum light bulbs. Standing in front of a lamp for a few minutes a day shifts both mood and energy levels. This lighting works too in treating Alzheimer's patients who suffer from depression when used at the dining room tables fitted with full spectrum bulbs on the surface. Exposure to essential natural light during meal times significantly improved their memory and mood.

Reconnecting with Nature and our place in it is essential for our health and well-being. Our technology-driven lifestyle disrupts this connection by keeping us indoors more than any time in human history, so the need is greater than ever. Be honest, how much are you outside on any given day?

An awareness of the environment and our place in it is a powerful way to manage the surrounding energy and our emotional and physical reactions to it. Opening our eyes to our surroundings gives us the power to create more of the life we want.

Chapter 15

ART AND SCIENCE OF HAPPINESS

I sat at the bottom of a deep well of depression after my sister died in 2006, drowning in guilt for not saving her, and in my family's pain despite being hundreds of miles apart. I'd promised her I'd live life fully, promised myself I'd make the most of every day and be joyful. For well over a year, I failed to keep my promise.

Business took my husband to Hawaii, and I went along for the ride. At a friend's urging, I signed up for a chartered boat service to go swimming with wild dolphins off the island of Oahu. Terrified, I lay awake the night before my scheduled adventure, obsessing about sharks and drowning because I didn't know how to snorkel.

The next morning, I forced myself to drive an hour to the marina, despite my fear. Once on the boat I chatted and laughed with the staff and other passengers, feigning confidence as we motored out to sea.

We stopped a hundred yards offshore to practice with the gear, so I awkwardly jumped in the water and put on my mask. Breathing hard and kicking frantically as visions of *Jaws* danced through my head, I put my face in the water and looked down. Rays of sunlight shot through the clear water illuminating a sandy bottom as a giant sea turtle paddled silently through the beams.

Time stopped. My breath slowed, and a wave, not of water but energy passed through me, deleting my thoughts as my mind scrambled to comprehend what I saw. I had no reference for such beauty and peace.

Dropping below the ocean's surface into this magical place stunned me into the submission that the mundane world I struggled with and clung to isn't all there is. At that moment, I lost my grandiosity and felt humbled and small. Here was a world that knows nothing about me, that lives and dies and exists independent of what I feel, see or think. I have no power here, no impact. My problems don't matter. There is wholeness apart from me, and it is real. I witnessed my version of God in the life force creating and permeating this beauty immense and breathtaking and felt one with that force emanating through me.

Depression left me that day and didn't return for nearly two years.

***

Happiness is a dirty word when we're in the pit of despair. We can't imagine what it's like to feel good, nor do you particularly like anyone else who looks happy. Perhaps if we look honestly enough at our thoughts and actions, we might find the conflicting belief we can't be satisfied, or no one will notice us. If we're happy, it looks to others as if we're doing just fine. No need for them to change, help, or apologize for past wrongdoing. Unconsciously we are committed to staying in pain.

Being in a dark place is a guaranteed way to let others know something is wrong, and they need to do something about it. It's a backward way of thinking, and it eventually makes people run the other way which only validates

Depression's belief of not being wanted or needed. But now we know that we can stop being a victim to get what we need. It takes willingness. Are you willing to be happy?

We can't judge ourselves too harshly for remembering the negative experiences of our lives more than the positive ones. Focusing on danger is encoded in our awareness to keep us surviving and evolving as a species. It's our human nature. Although neuroscience proves we're hard-wired to remember negative experiences as a survival mechanism, studies show we are not doomed to a negative life. Because of neuroplasticity in our brains, it's possible to re-wire the neural pathways and experience more happiness. In other words, we can get off the path of depression and choose a new one through our actions.

We must rise above our physical nature in this way and rely on our spiritual nature. Connecting to our awareness of Soul and Spirit leads to beneficial action that creates positive experiences. They go hand in hand, and it is the stuff of the Soul that makes us happy.

In *Hardwiring Happiness: The New Brain Science of Contentment, Calm, and Confidence*[1], author Rick Hanson writes "if positive experiences (1) are intense enough (2) are novel enough, (3) occur often enough, or (4) if we direct our focused attention to them long enough, they will strengthen the brain's "happiness" neural pathways and therefore make it easier for us to feel positive emotions."

Practicing mindfulness or meditation, and spending time in nature are two activities that fit the criteria for re-wiring by creating positive experiences.

I undoubtedly benefited from the power of a new, intense experience during my trip to Hawaii. I often reflect on the magical turtle surrounded by light when

I feel sad to reactivate that neural pathway and energy vibration, and the incredible feeling that went with it.

Courageously doing things we've always longed to do but were too afraid is just the sort of new positive experience that directly impacts our capacity for happiness. With focused attention, and doing uplifting things regularly, we change the patterns worn into our brain, just as shifting our thoughts lifts us out of entrenched negative thinking.

In a recent study, Millennials (those born from 1982 to 2004) were asked, "What are your major life goals?" Almost 80% responded "to get rich," and another 50% included "to be famous." However, the things we chase for happiness don't make us happy at all. In fact, the more affluent the society, the more people suffer from depression and other mental and emotional dysfunction. It's easy to see then why the United States, and especially younger generations are experiencing depression and anxiety at unprecedented levels.

Turning this around is where caring for our Soul comes into play. Pursuing experiences and feelings we love, despite material or societal expectations means we're more likely to be happy.

Research also shows that happier societies are those who rank lower in income and are forced to share resources. This enforced need to share and help each other survive creates a community and fosters the sense of belonging.

It's been shown that more than anything, relationships keep us happier and healthier and sustain a longer, more satisfying life.

It harkens back to a primal need for a tribe, an unwavering community of friends and family who feed and protect us and need us in return. Deep down in us all, there is the desire to belong. How much of our depression stems from this sense of being cut off not only from ourselves but others?

Feeling sensitive and suffering from sadness to any degree forces us into isolation. Often it's too hard to be around people, but we still need these interactions to learn about ourselves. Through the contact and conflict of relating to others, we learn to bring up and identify feelings, to hear how we think, and see how we act in different situations. We develop our personality and our character. We need the real-life feedback of other people as our mirrors because they reflect an aspect of us and act as a gift to learn what we might change to live more authentically. This doesn't apply to only the "negative" stuff in others we encounter, but also things the unique, creative, kind, funny, smart people in your life reflect about you too. Anyone or anything you are drawn to and appreciate lives in you as a light shadow mirroring a positive aspect.

We need to engage and relate to others in any way we can for our personal growth. We can't see ourselves unless we're being reflected by others. Speaking to strangers as we go about our days or taking any opportunity to meet new people and widen our circle lets us see ourselves in a new light. We learn by who shows up in our life because they are a mirror of us.

The greatest advantage of engaging in relationships is the opportunity to give to others. Giving is one of those positive activities hard-wired into our behavior because it keeps the tribe together on a primal level. When you do something for someone else, you not only get rewarded by group approval, but you activate the "feel good" neurochemical dopamine in your brain. Feeling good ensures that the tribe survives.

But, there's a vast difference between over-giving and exhaustive over-doing out of obligation or the fear of not being liked, as opposed to giving from your heart. As you listen to intuition and the needs of your Soul you discriminate between giving from a place of guilt or fear and an honest sense of service flowing through you. You give from a place of love when you love what you're doing. This healthy way of giving fills you up too. When you're clear about your gifts and what you bring to the world soulfully, doing for others is a powerful reflection of your best self. Consider how you can be part of your neighborhood or community "tribe," and even the whole human tribe in a way that nourishes you too.

When you're willing to be of service, something new comes through you, and people and the world respond in kind. You make connections. You see value in your presence and feel empowered to create change for the better.

For example, my friend Jamie works at an unfulfilling corporate job where she often feels unable to be her authentic self. Wanting to feel more joyful at work, she recently started her day with a meditative prayer, asking she be open to being of service in any way the Universe saw fit.

Throughout the day, three of her co-workers sought her out, asking her advice on professional or deeply personal issues. She got the chance to share her gift of compassionate listening, and to offer guidance and support rooted in personal growth and spirituality that makes others feel seen and heard. On that day, she made a difference to others and saw how she could bring more of herself and what makes her happy to the world at work. It started by asking and then being open to what comes.

When we're on the right track, positive feedback from our outer environment appears in ways we don't expect; just like Jamie's coworkers all seeking her out on the same day in lovely synchronicity.

We have the power to be happier. Science supports that the art of happiness is something we can practice if we're willing. Willingness comes when we align with our spiritual self to find the courage we need to act. Like any art, it requires patience and practice to get better.

Because feeling happy wasn't natural, I created a visual representation of what I call my "Four-Fold Happiness Plan" – a grand title for the list of simple activities and insights I've built into my daily life to cultivate happiness. It's taped to my office wall to remind me when I feel myself slipping into a funk: Oh yeah, this is what I need to do.

This plan synthesizes the influential work of others with what I know works in a way that can be quickly understood. It validates that the activities and behaviors that are good for me personally are the same things that cultivate universal happiness.

My brain needs this connection between ideas, and when I see the same small actions framed in different ways, I'm thrilled that what works is doable. As my friend Laura often says, "Small hinges move big doors." This work isn't rocket science – I can do this!

I can get lost in the lofty ideas of others and need a framework to make them practical and real. To see the connection between what I believe and what others were telling me to do to help myself. What a relief to have this prescription for a happier life in front of me. I don't have to keep reinventing the wheel. These are the things to do. It's the same thing, a different angle. Same way, a new day.

The plan reminds me I have a choice through my action to have more happiness in my life. I'm not a victim with no control. It really is just that simple – do certain things, even if you don't want to, and you will feel better. The old saying "fake it until you make it" actually works on a biological, and emotional level.

Remembering my plan and acting on it is the "medicine" I use daily to be who I want to be, feel how I want to feel, and live how I want to live. Some days it tastes wonderful, and I take it willingly, other days I force it down my throat knowing it is what I must do to keep my head above water and out of despair.

The Four-Fold Happiness Plan looks like this:

NECESSITIES	FYYBR
• READ • WRITE • MEDITATE • MOVE	• WISDOM • HEART • COURAGE
HOW TO BE HAPPY DAILY	**AWAKENED DOING**
• SEND THANKS OR PRAISE TO SOMEONE • RANDOM ACT OF KINDNESS • 15 MINUTE EXERCISE • TWO MINUTE BALANCE – BREATHING • GRATEFULLNESS – WRITE THREE THINGS	• ACCEPTANCE • ENJOYMENT • ENTHUSIASM

The First Quadrant - Necessities

There are four things I must do in some combination consistently to keep myself "sane" and happy. Even if I only do them for a few minutes, it matters. My goal is to start every day with one of these necessities.

How did I come to choose these things? It started with asking myself what makes me genuinely happy? What activities naturally make me feel better when I do them? These are the things I consistently reach for, some since childhood, to comfort myself and shift my mood or experience. They are a foundation of my existence and keep me in touch with the person I am at my core. These necessities are my 'big medicine' and heal me time and time again. And, not surprisingly, they are proven methods to help anyone shift.

READ. Reading something positive, inspirational or exciting shifts my perspective. "Reading" people as a psychic is my passion. I see the meaning behind the themes and characters in stories of others' lives they've intentionally created as Spirit.

WRITE. Putting words on paper to express my heart or empty my mind is an essential part of my nature. It doesn't have to be good writing. I have to write stuff down; whether it's a to-do list, a mental rant, or a grand vision of life and the world, it's all fulfilling.

MEDITATE. I need my space and quiet. We all do, but it's especially true when you are energetically sensitive to the world around you. Any time I am still I remember my essence.

MOVE. Moving my body moves energy and shifts my emotions. I walk, do Pilates, stretch, or get up from my desk and let my body break into a spontaneous dance. I read once you can't feel depressed if you stand up with your arms open wide above you. Try it!

The Second Quadrant - Follow Your Yellow Brick Road

As a Kansas girl, Dorothy's story in the movie The Wizard of Oz resonates deeply with me, but it is the story for all of us seeking wholeness. It reminds us that on the road of life we need only our banished companions of Wisdom, Heart, and Courage to get home to wholeness.

Waking up to our inherent spiritual power and wisdom moves us out of being "hung up" by doubt, ignorance, and isolation. It's only after the Scarecrow gets his feet on the ground that he taps into his answers and knows without knowing how he knows.

Through the guidance of our inner wisdom, we come to meet our Heart. The seat of compassion, love, kindness. It's here we find our emotional, sensitive self. Like the Tinman, the anxious overwhelmed one who feels everything despite the armor. The Heart is the core of who we are and links heaven and Earth. Heart tells us what we value, what we love, and what we long for through our Soul's language. What wants to be rediscovered, revealed, released? We find our Heart through wisdom, which validates trust in ourselves.

As trust builds, we become willing to face our fear and discover the Courage to act on our behalf. Courage is not fearlessness; it's authenticity with fear at your side. There is no need to cover it up like the Cowardly Lion, a blustery fake who runs the other way when life gets hard. We don't wait to be fearless; we just try to be sincere. We cry our tears and move forward, knowing we'll feel proud when we do.

The Yellow Brick Road is a powerful reminder: I do know. Trust in love. Act, even if I'm afraid.

The Third Quadrant - Cultivate Happiness

I'm trying to grow my happiness daily, so I cultivate each day like a farmer, breaking up the soil of my over-worked routines and planting new behaviors that feed me the feelings I want to feel.

I've borrowed seeds of good habits from Shawn Achor's *21 Days to Happiness*[2] plan to cultivate happiness by reaching out to others with a positive intention and performing random acts of kindness. Both habits incorporate feelings of empowered service and push the dopamine button by connecting us to others.

I combine happiness habits to get more bang for my buck. I know breathing in the beauty of the sun, moon or stars cultivates mindfulness and presence and being outside is the perfect place to exercise. Taking just 15 minutes a day to walk or ride bike improves mood even more. These are conscious choices available to practice when you're feeling good and when you're not. It doesn't require that you are not depressed to do any of them but doing them helps move you to a better place.

I keep a small "success journal" next to my bed where I can't ignore it and end each day jotting down at least three ways I succeeded. It's my twist on a gratitude list. I note successes large and small, anything from not complaining to a slow grocery clerk, eating only three cookies instead of half the package, or signing on a new long-term client. Many nights my first entry is "I'm writing in this journal even though I don't want to" when I am tired and or feeling like a kid who doesn't want to do her homework.

Finding success at the end of every day helps me see myself in a more positive light overall. I've stopped believing I don't accomplish enough and that I'm nowhere near where I "should" be with my goals. Every little success is proof that I'm growing and blossoming into the person I want to look like, sound like, and most of all feel like. It brings me closer to harvesting the bigger vision I hold for my life.

The Fourth Quadrant - Stay Awake

Years of depression made me adept at not feeling anything. Now I strive to stay awake to my feelings by listening to my thoughts and conversing with my banished parts. I settle into feeling my feelings instead of looking for ways to tamp them down or keep them at bay. I stay awake by asking myself questions. How do I feel right now? Pay attention and notice. It doesn't mean you have to do anything, the noticing usually makes a shift.

Philosopher Eckhart Tolle says that to stay aligned with the creative power of the universe we must strive to consciously be in a state of acceptance, enjoyment, or enthusiasm about our circumstances. It is our state of consciousness that determines how we do anything in life.[3]

Noticing if I am in a state of acceptance, enjoyment, or enthusiasm sets an intention for my awareness to take me where I want to go. It gives me a clear definition to check myself against, and then do what I can to raise my emotional and energetic vibration. To have a talk with myself or switch gears when what I'm doing isn't working out. Usually, I find that I need to stop fighting reality. When I do, it's easier to feel better and move to a more aligned state.

I use a daily planner by Danielle La Porte to keep me focused on my feelings while I work and play at creating a successful life. The front cover is emblazoned with the words "What I Will Do To Feel the Way I Want To Feel"[4] in bright gold, and the calendar inside is filled with reminders of positive feelings and the power to choose. When I consciously choose how I want to feel and aspire to cultivating those feelings, my daily to-do list tells me it is not only what I do, but how to frame my actions with intention as I do it. I plan my days around actions that make me feel that way. I choose words like accomplished, balanced, focused and create a plan for the day that brings me what I need.

The Four-Fold Plan organized on paper helps me see the connection between ideas and adds layers of understanding to what works for me and why. I've read many things over the years and drawn from others work to inspire and save me. I've integrated what feels right into my life from many paths that re-state and amplify the same goal. I need different perspectives to reach all aspects of my inner life that have been committed to staying in Depression. Different voices ring true to different parts of me.

I seek the wisdom of others and find the connections. It's comforting to see the same ideas expressed over and over in a new way. It gives me a foundation and shows me there is a core to happiness I can keep going back to. It is within reach, it is within me. I'm standing on sacred ground.

Chapter 16

THE POWER OF PLACE

For eons, people recognized the energy of an environment imbued by the gods or spirits inhabiting that place. They chose living spaces based on the favorability of that energy, on the lay of the land, the proximity and relationship to water, and how weather moved across the geography.

Intuitively, we know if a home or building feels comfortable or not the minute we walk through the door. We pick up the "vibe" of a place – the energy or life force created by the people or things within that environment. Any real estate agent will tell us how powerful this sense is. People choose a home or office space based more on how it feels than anything else.

Through our energy, we reflect our surroundings, and our surroundings reflect us. As an energetically sensitive person observing the world, how you create your home environment is crucial. Look around with an unbiased eye. What does where you live and what surrounds you say about you and the story of your life as you experience it?

The ancient art of *feng shui* recognizes this inner/outer reflection and gives us a system for understanding how our emotional, physical, mental, and spiritual state is affected by both our natural and created environments. The precursor to modern architectural and interior design, feng shui strives for alignment through balance and beauty.

I use what I call Intuitive feng shui to shift myself and my family out of a rut, like poor health, drama at school, or a need for more clients, money or fun. It is one way I can take control of things outside of myself to shift how I feel on the inside. Stepping back with an objective eye to my home lets me find clues to what's going on inside of me – the source of my blahs or frustrations, a sticking point keeping me from moving forward with a project or enjoying relationships.

You don't have to understand or even believe in feng shui principles to know that clearing and cleaning your home has an immediate impact on how it feels and how you feel. Forgotten things and forgotten places are like forgotten parts of ourselves. It's important to bring them to light and tend to them. Everything holds energy, and the longer things sit gathering dust, neglected and outdated, the more oppressive the energy becomes.

It's easy to let little nuisances wear on us, like an energetic poke in the eye with a stick, and we don't even realize it. We endure daily irritations at home that unconsciously remind us of our procrastination and failure, like the doorknob that doesn't work, grimy handprints around the light switch, a burned-out bulb, or that damn rug you keep tripping over. We stop noticing the dust bunnies, the weeds in the backyard, and ignore the junk drawer or junk closet (or junk room!); even if it drives us crazy. And let's not even talk about the garage! When we lose sight of our intention and energy, we fall asleep to what surrounds us. Eventually what should feel like a sanctuary to us no longer supports our best self and feels like home.

Noticing the state of our home, office, and the garden is a powerful first step to change how we think, feel, and ultimately, the quality of our life. Feng shui uses the octagon shaped ba-gua which consists of trigrams representing universally important life interests – Career, Knowledge, Family, Wealth, Fame, Relationships, Creativity, Travel/Benefactors, and Health. Like a roadmap, the ba-gua can be superimposed over the floorplan of a house or room to find what area of the home corresponds to a particular life category, and a to diagnose what is working and what's not in your life and why (See Appendix).

Water, wood, fire, earth, and metal make up everything around us even in human-made environments, but the combination or type of elements, and how they are placed in the home or office, profoundly influence us. Over the last 125 years our jobs and lifestyle have increasingly cut us off from natural surroundings, and it's only getting worse. Although the trend is changing, most corporate settings are designed to separate and standardize; there's not a lot of life in neutral color schemes and materials. Low ceilings, windowless rooms, artificial lights, and processed air do nothing to invigorate our bodies.

Looking at the energetic factors influenced by color, objects, and the natural elements (water, wood, fire, earth, metal) present in each section of the ba-gua as it relates to your house reveals possible problems impacting the flow of "chi" or life force energy in the home. Then by intentionally creating a physical "cure" using corrective colors, elements, and symbols of our desires, the environment shifts energetically, which brings healing and change.

Often during a reading, I am clairvoyantly drawn to a client's home. In my mind's eye, I see and feel the energy of a particular room that relates to the questions or challenges we're discussing. When I ask, "What does this room look like?" there is always a direct correlation.

For example, Jane asked why she has so much trouble charging full value for her marketing services and getting her clients to pay on time. My attention drew to the rear left corner of her house which felt, as I sensed into it, cold and lifeless. This corner is the wealth space, the area of her home where money, prosperity, and abundance are reflected and supported. When I asked her to describe this part of her house, she said it was the living room, but she "hated the color on the walls" and didn't spend much time there. There were a few plants, one of them dying, a fireplace she never used, and the furniture wasn't very comfortable. She'd been thinking about re-painting and buying new furniture for some time but couldn't seem to decide. Unclear about what to do, she feared buying the wrong things so didn't act on what she wanted at all.

It's no surprise she found it difficult to ask for what she wanted and keep money flowing easily. She had pulled all her attention and energy out of her wealth and let herself falter with indecision. Her home reflected what was going on in her life; discomfort, the wrong "color" of clients who didn't appreciate her, a slowly dying client list. Her social life had dwindled too, and she wasn't getting out or having fun when she did see friends

As homework, I challenged Jane to boldly graffiti the things that represent abundance to her in big letters on the ugly living room walls and live with it for a week to clearly see the things she wanted more of in her life. Doing so would not only imbue her intention and desire into the physical walls of her home, but also motivate her to buy the paint and get busy creating real change. As we talked she confessed to finding a sofa she loved but left it in an online shopping cart unpurchased because she felt she didn't deserve it. Her next assignment then was to declare what she wanted by buying the sofa and clear out the old furniture and plants to make room for new energy and life.

Two weeks later Jane reported that the troublesome client paid their invoice in full and that they had mutually ended the business relationship. Jane felt relieved to be free of her burdensome client and ready to find the clients with whom she was excited to work.

You become an energy worker when you approach your home with an intentional frame of mind. Ask yourself: What can I let go? What feels stuck here? What makes me annoyed, angry, irritated, sad? What do I want to bring more of into my life? Take a section of your home or a room and sort through the clutter, get rid of worn-out things, or objects that evoke feelings you don't want to feel. Making a noticeable shift in the energy of your home, and thus your life doesn't have to cost a lot of money or time.

My friend Lilly has a family room full of old furniture she can't afford to replace. It also is in her "wealth space," the section of her home that represents and holds energy for abundance. She knew she wanted to enliven the space and bring in her creativity, so instead of focusing on what wasn't working and waiting to buy new furniture, she cleared and filed the piles of paperwork on her desk, dusted her computer, and opened the window blinds part way to let in more sunshine. She cut several lovely flowers from her yard and put them in a vase. The light caught the color and the water, inspiring her with serene beauty.

In less than an hour, her family room transformed from a place where she only saw what was wrong into a comfortable spot where she could be at home. Now she's excited about sitting at her desk and getting back to the forgotten creative business projects to make more money.

Repeatedly I go into the nooks and crannies of my home and yard to work out the rough edges of my life. Sometimes it takes years to get to it (that garage!) but what a difference it makes when you do. The principle of timing applies here too. When you're ready to work a particular issue or area of your life, you'll get to it, and things will move quickly and easily.

Intuitive feng shui speaks to the power of symbol, ritual, and acting with intention when looking at life and how to move it in the direction you want it to go.

If you want more of a good thing in your life, you must make room for it. Just as you clear the space in your aura for your unique energy, so it is for your home and the larger energetic field where you live. Be selective. Don't keep things out of guilt, don't buy stuff you don't need, or hang on to things you don't use or want. Shifting your mindset this way is good for you, and even more so for the planet as you move away from the "consume, consume, consume" mentality of our culture toward a thoughtful attitude. Re-purpose what you can, share or give away, donate, recycle. It is all moving energy positively; dynamic, giving, and uplifting.

Chapter 17

BE YOUR OWN FENG SHUI EXPERT

Feng shui means "wind and water," the natural movement of elements across the earth, and the life force they carry. Both are essential, but too much of either can be devastating.

Using just the basic tenets of this complex and richly symbolic system can improve your environment and well-being. You don't have to delve too deep into feng shui to use its principles to your advantage. Here's how to remove what's not working and bring in what does to raise your energy vibration to a more positive state at home or work.

Clear It Out

You know it; you hate it, but it must be done. It's time to clear things out. Clutter is a double feng shui nightmare. It takes up valuable space that is better used for energy and people to move freely or to provide blank space for your eyes and mind to rest and process. Clutter blocks the flow of energy and creates pools of stagnant or 'dead' energy in the form of memories, irritations, or irrelevance, not to mention dust. Take a slow, objective look at your home or workspace to look for clutter holding energy, emotions and more. Ask yourself questions:

Are your drawers full of clothes you don't wear or information you've held to follow up, but never have?

How much of your clutter do you keep out of fear that you might need it "someday," or out of guilt because it cost a lot or was a gift?

Are you surrounded by electronic clutter? The constant whirring and buzzing of devices and appliances also fill up space with vibrations we unconsciously respond to all day. First and foremost, get rid of the TV in the bedroom.

Perhaps you have too much of a "good" thing.

Are your walls covered with family photos or shelves crammed with awards or mementos?

Do family heirlooms and documents take up too much of your space, keeping your energy stuck in the past?

Have you created distractions by surrounding yourself with things that hurt your focus and concentration?

Purge, be selective. Like a river, energy needs to circulate through and around your home or business, clearing and bringing in a new life with ideas, physical energy, health and abundance of all kinds. The more space, the more the river of life can flow. Clear, then clean. Honestly, when's the last time you wiped off your desk or vacuumed under the bed?

Fix It

When you look around your home or office, ask yourself these questions:

Is there something you react to negatively every time you see it? That light that flickers and hums overhead, a squeaky chair.

Do you walk around boxes or duck your head?

What do you see that makes you cringe? The project you didn't finish, the color of the walls?

What makes you feel angry?

Annoyances big and small create negativity inside you, and around you. Left unattended, they eventually become subconscious reactions and set the tone for a room or home. You simmer in a stew of frustration! You may no longer know what makes you irritated and still feel annoyed every time you walk into the room.

Whatever the issue, make it a priority to deal with it once and for all. You'll probably find it doesn't take much effort to resolve something you've been avoiding for so long.

Fill It Up

Once you've cleared out any space in your home, garden or office, it's essential to fill it back up with positive things. Feng shui uses natural elements and color to balance the energy of the environment, thus creating balance in your life experiences. Even without knowing the exact positions of your space as it relates to the ba-gua, you can use these primary principles to improve the energy of your home or business.

The following elements and colors correspond to the ba-gua and activate the supportive power for those same areas of your life:

CAREER—Water—Black

KNOWLEDGE—Blue

FAMILY—Wood—Green

WEALTH—Purple

FAME—Fire—Red

RELATIONSHIPS—Pink
CREATIVITY/CHILDREN—Metal—White
BENEFACTORS/TRAVEL—Gray
HEALTH—Earth—Yellow

Bring in Color

Research proves what people living closer to nature a thousand years ago knew, namely that color influences emotional and physical well-being. Yet we spend much of our time in business settings, schools, and apartment buildings with dull neutral tones that lower the vibration of an environment and wash out creativity.

Color has power. In feng shui terms, fiery red stokes imagination and confidence, and blue encourages knowledge and enlightenment. Green symbolizes growth, new beginnings, and promotes strong family and community ties. Bring pops of color in to enliven your senses, to move your attention and eye around the space, and to lift your spirits.

Keep in mind you don't have to repaint your house or have a patchwork décor reflecting the ba-gua. You can use colors in the same tones as the supportive color, or hide the color behind furniture, in closets, or under the bed. Bring in artwork or decorative objects that have the color within them. For example, relationships are important to all of us, but not many want to have a room full of pink (the color that supports the relationship area of your home). If your relationship space happens to be in your bedroom, you can use garnet or fuchsia sheets under your usual comforter, or keep two red roses by the bedside to symbolize love and connection while adding the color vibration you want. Or create a collage of words or pictures on pink colored paper signifying what you want in all of your relationships, then tuck it in your nightstand drawer.

Bring in Elements

Combine color with natural elements like wood, earth, fire, water, and metal. Candles symbolize fire which supports self-esteem and promotes recognition from others. Use pictures of mountains to ground a chaotic space, or to support health in the center area of your home. A small water fountain is both soothing and energizing, and moving water symbolizes prosperity. Use it in the front and center section of your home or office to support positive movement in your life and career.

If you are struggling in a particular area of your life, look to see if the supportive element is present. Or, check for dominance of another element that may be hindering positive energy. For example, my client Lena skipped from job to job looking for a place to grow and be promoted. She never seemed to gain any traction in her career, and felt her "real" life was waiting for her somewhere out in the future. The "career" section of her home, which also represents the overall life path, revealed why.

The entrance to her door is located in this area, at the front and center of the house. From outside large overgrown bushes (wood) blocked the view, making it difficult to see the house (and symbolically her as well). Heavy pots (earth) devoid of plants created a wall along the porch, further stopping the flow of lifeforce energy into her home, and therefore her life. The sidewalk, porch, and the exterior walls of the house were the same dull terracotta color and were covered with dust and cobwebs. Inside the house next to the front door a shelf held a dusty collection of crystals and rocks near a large brick fireplace (earth). The preponderance of the earth element energetically dammed up what should be the flowing energy of water in the "career" area of her home.

To bring movement and vitality back into her career and her life path, she cut back the landscaping, removed the pots and swept, and painted her front door a lovely dark blue, the color of deep water. Inside, she pared down and cleaned her rock collection and moved it toward the center of the house where it belonged elementally. She placed a small water fountain in the living room near the door to remind her of the flow of life moving through her. She added more supportive blue and water to her career area by hanging photos of Lake Tahoe, a place she loves and hopes to retire to. She made a point to leave the blinds open to both let light and life in and to give herself an expanded view of her world.

A few weeks later, Lena saw an interesting brochure for a management certification program through a local university. She proposed taking the class to her employer, pointing out how she could help the company be more successful in the long run and asked if they would be willing to pay for the class. After completing the course, she found a new direction for her passion and established herself as a valuable asset to her company. She felt energized about her work, herself, and the possibilities life had to offer.

Bring in Life

Live plants are a quick and inexpensive solution to enhance the energy of any space. Even if you're not a green thumb, there are plenty of low maintenance plants happy to live with you with little attention.

Many plants act as natural air filters to process environmental toxins and convert carbon dioxide to oxygen. Plants add color and natural vibrancy. Use them to block unwanted views, to divert the flow of foot traffic or energy away from you in a busy area, or to lift the energy in dead spots with their constant upward growth.

Plants contribute to the healthy energy of an environment, and also indicate when the energy is out of balance. Struggling plants reflect struggling inhabitants. Feng shui Master Karen Cooper tells how one of her clients struggled with depression and poor health long after the loss of her husband. Upon entering her home, Karen noticed numerous potted plants throughout the house withering away in cramped plastic containers. When Karen asked why she kept them, her client explained the plants were all memorial gifts from her husband's funeral. She felt obligated to take them home and keep them. Karen explained that although her intentions were good, the plants were a constant reminder of her grief and sorrow, and carried the energy of that day. She asked her client to let go and compost the weakest of the plants, and choose just a few of the healthiest ones to re-pot in new soil with nutrients and room to grow that would represent her own new growth and healthier life.

Karen's client felt an immediate lightness in her home as they gathered up the dying plants and took them outside. Not long after her exhaustion disappeared. She felt vital and enthused about her own life once she stopped trying to sustain a life that no longer existed. Now her plants are a healthy reminder of her husband, and a symbol that life continues and grows in unimaginable ways if nurtured.

Surround Yourself with Your Self

Intuitive feng shui creates an environment that reflects our true Self, that part of us that innately knows what we need to align with the universal life force that moves us toward happiness. Addressing daily challenges or accomplishing goals requires focus, confidence and a sense of purpose. It's far easier to recognize your purpose by surrounding yourself with positive reminders of what makes you happy; what makes you, you.

My client Natalie is a spunky, single woman who worked hard to help build a small business and own her own home. At 45, she decided she wanted to enjoy having a serious relationship with someone who she could spend the rest of her life with. She dated a lot through the years but found herself drawn to younger or immature men who not interested in commitment. She was unhappy with her current boyfriend who wasn't working and didn't have much drive and needed support to end the relationship and move on.

Her neat little bungalow reflected her quirky humor and a love of all things Hawaiian. In the kitchen, there was a collection of salt and pepper shakers and a Kit-Cat Klock with a swinging tail and roving eyes adorned the walls. A tiki-bar sat ready for service just outside the sliding door in the dining room. Artwork and seashells collected on her trips to the islands were tastefully placed throughout the living room. But walking into her bedroom was like stepping back in time. Her bed was covered in a baby pink comforter that looked like it once belonged to her grandma. At least 30 small stuffed animals rested against the pillows, backed by a huge stuffed bear. Posters from concerts and sporting events she attended as a teenager plastered one wall. She loved this stuff – she thought it was cute.

I gently pointed out the discrepancy between what she said she wanted, and what was reflected unconsciously by her the décor of her room. This was the room of a 13-year-old girl, not that of a mature woman wanting a strong, lasting relationship. Fortunately, Natalie could laugh at herself and be open to creating a "grown-up" room that reflected her true self, and the kind of intimate relationship she wanted. She sold her furniture to buy something more modern and took time sorting and saving the best of her memorabilia. She enjoyed finding new homes for the stuffed animals by sharing them with children from her church. She chose a deep purple comforter to replace the little girl pink, evoking the richness and comfort of a royal robe. She brought in new bedside lamps and scented candles to create a restful ambiance at night.

Within a few months, she comfortably ended her relationship for good and decided to spend time doing more inner work before seeking out a partner. She slept better at night, feeling supported by her decision and her power as a mature woman to take care of herself.

Your home should be your sanctuary, with areas of both restful and enlivened energy. All of which can be done simply, authentically, in a way that reflects you and your family's personality and soul. This is not about having more, or trendy stuff to be in style. But often your home needs to change and grow with you as you mature and deepen through life experiences and understanding. What served you at one time may not hold true years later.

Objects you find beautiful or memorable in a positive way help set the tone for the energetic environment you want to inhabit. But keep the present in mind. If I walked into your home would I know who you are now? Who you aspire to be?

Chapter 18

LIGHTNESS

Libby, a single mom with two boys and a combative ex-husband, had been in a downward spiral for over a year. In the space of four months her favorite uncle died suddenly, she was laid off from her job, and her boyfriend who'd been her best friend for years ended their relationship.

Overwhelmed by loss and unable to find work in her field, Libby fell deep into depression, gaining fifty pounds "without noticing." She came to see me only after her concerned sister gave her a reading as a gift.

She appeared withdrawn and meek, afraid to take up space. Petite and pretty with a great smile and a splattering of freckles, it was clear as soon as I tapped into her energy field she was holding back and covering an immensely creative life force.

As Spirit she looked like a magnificent and loving goddess surrounded by emerald green energy emitting a deep love for Nature. She had an intuitive understanding of the Earth's ability to heal, and a sincere desire to share it. But, she'd cut herself off from this innate wisdom, which now was leading her back to it by shaking up her life enough to make her switch directions. It was clear her

intention this lifetime is to connect herself and others to
Nature to heal themselves and to protect our planet by
understanding a loving connection with it.

After describing how I saw her, Libby explained she
had been working as a geologist in a job that dealt more
with paperwork and numbers than being close to the
Earth. She loves stones and studying the healing proper-
ties of crystals and rocks but stopped reading her books
on the subject. Hiking and photographing nature are
her favorite pastimes, but she had given those up too as
motherhood and depression consumed her days. She'd
lost all connection and drive to pursue the things she
loves and feed her soul.

Within two days of our first session, she was contacted
to teach as a substitute for the first time, ending nearly a
year of unemployment. In the coming months, she discovered she loved working with the kids and found them
energizing and fun. She took time to walk in nature and
take photos, even daring to share them on social media.
She found an old notebook and wrote poetry again.

Weeks later we talked about intense psychic experiences
she disregarded throughout her life; her encounters with
loved ones who had passed away and the unexpressed
energy of anger from emotional abuse that had gone
underground and buried her creativity.

As part of her homework, she committed to clearing
out her garage to make space and let go of old things.
While she worked her neighbor showed up, and Libby
dared to confront her about how she always parked on
Libby's side of the garage and took up more space with
her belongings. After the encounter, she felt proud of
herself, no longer victimized. In the coming weeks, she
found it easier to say what she needed and get it. Even her

ex-husband, not one to do her any favors, remembered her birthday and offered to let her have the boys on what was always "his day," and sent a cake along home with them. She was floored.

Each time she took care of something her Soul longed for, each time she listened and took a small step to do something for herself, she felt better. What's more, the world around her seemed to magically respond to support and give her what she wanted, or as she discovered, what she needed.

Today Libby is fit, healthy and strong. She's back in school finishing a new degree to become a full-time science teacher, and her boys are thriving finding their talents in sports and school. By combining what her soul loves, she's unearthed her purpose: to teach others about the beauty and power of nature and the need to enjoy it, explore it and save it. Doing so heals her and others, just as her Spirit intended when embarking on this life.

Living in the Light

Depression is the teacher that redirects us toward our purpose. It is the red flag that warns us we aren't listening to our Soul.

Depression's wish for us is to find our light. That's why it fights so hard to stay with us – it knows that the deeper we are carved with sorrow, the more joy we can contain.[1] When we understand this, we become the well to draw from in all circumstances of our life.

Living with Depression is an ongoing journey. It's the practice of staying awake and aware, and it is a gift. Depression teaches us how to see in the dark.

When we've suffered trauma or deep emotional pain early in our lives, it can feel odd and vulnerable to step into the light of our spiritual wholeness. We may recall times of feeling happy and trusting, as children deserve to be, only to be hit by disappointment, betrayal, or violence. Over the years, we grew accustomed to the heaviness of depression and wore it like a thick robe of protection.

But by tapping into the things that make us happy, or drawing from uplifting memories to recall what happiness feels like in the body, we can drop that heavy robe for an instant to test the waters and grow accustomed to its freedom before putting it back on again. We can learn to think, *It's okay if I'm happy. Nothing terrible will come.*

When depression returns, we have places to go inside us to draw strength and guidance. We have easy, practical actions to take even when we feel bound up by Depression's weighty demands.

We discover the willingness to change and the power to do so by giving ourselves credit for every small thing that moves us down the path of wisdom, heart, and courage. If our feet slip out from under us when grief, loss, anger, disappointment, and pain come calling, we reach for reminders and tools to steady us again, knowing it is okay to welcome all feelings.

Until now, we defined ourselves by our painful story, recounting things that were done to us, who was to blame for the state of our life. At every opportunity for happiness, we reminded ourselves of why it can't be.

But, what we make the challenges of life mean is within our control, how we respond to our feelings and then act upon them is up to us. Embracing radical acceptance of ourselves and the inevitability of life challenges opens us to the possibility of joy.

We are the author of our stories. Ever-increasing awareness about our thoughts, feelings, and desires gives us more choice at any moment and lets us rewrite our story from that point on. And with this new insight, we behave differently. We become the hero and heroine of our own life story.

By now you've glimpsed your Self, a radiant being indistinguishable from all of life and the perfection in Nature. You've seen the potential present in you at all times, like an oak tree within an acorn that only requires the right soil and conditions to sprout and grow.[2]

It's been there since before your birth. You've known all along what to do and how to do it. You've planned this lifetime to learn and chose hardship as a necessary means of experience, understanding your Spirit is infinitely greater than any fleeting emotional suffering. You are endless and always moving toward understanding and growth. Conflict creates us. It makes us better when we learn from it. It drives us toward peace.

By listening to your thoughts and feelings, you seek to remember who you are in as many moments in the day as possible. To be present in the tangible world around you and wholly conscious of the light humming inside. Remember who you are by listening to all parts of you so you can discern the intuitive language of your Soul.

You remember who you are by settling into the home of your body, and by creating a home for Depression for you to come and go as you need.

And by connecting to the greater body of the earth, you find yourself at home in the world.

You are now a spiritual activist. By activating an awakened presence of Spirit, you take responsibility for your personal space. You open to the majestic force of creative consciousness that wants to move through you positively. By being more of YOU, you contribute to the world in a better way.

You uplift and enrich your space, your home, then your community and the world by contributing positive, peaceful and purposeful energy into the world. You are an activist for what is beautiful and right. Activating your spiritual consciousness creates an intimate connection between you and all living beings, clarifying that the planet is yours to take care of too.

Open to the idea we are all one. Everything is one. As you take responsibility for the energy around you, set your space. In this way, you combat hate, judgment, fear. As you save yourself, you help save the world, and that is purpose enough to be here. Your contribution is being you.

And yet, you will descend, but you have a way out.

Despite years of seeking and studying, of reading and writing, Depression still visits me. It's important to share because for so long I judged myself for it. I feared being found out. How could someone calling herself a spiritual healer have dark times? How can I help someone else if I can't help myself?

But that is our sole purpose, our Soul purpose. We who are drawn to darkness and healing. That is our life; going down and coming back. Going down and coming back, each time knowing something new.

We go down, and we come back, and when we do, we bring one more part of ourselves with us. It is the journey of departing and returning that we are learning to make the most of, how simply, to return.

The goal *is* the return. The healing and the message and the purpose are in the ascent. It's the opportunity to ask, "How do I make my way back? How do I share it and bring life back with me?"

Life comes from death and darkness. If we fulfill our natural destiny, it is to keep being reborn. We, as the depressed, are the wise people carrying the lantern back from the underground. With awareness and willingness, we navigated the labyrinth, and because we did not give up – because we keep seeking – we have learned the way. We light the path for others to return.

We are the way – showers. The healers and lightworkers. Each time we go down and come back, we save ourselves, and a piece of the world. There is no greater gift than this. It's why we are here.

It is more than enough.

Say it out loud:

I Am Enough!

Appendix

Grounding Meditation

1.   Sit comfortably with your eyes closed and your feet flat on the ground and take three deep breaths.

2.   Drop your awareness down to the base of your spine at the tailbone, noticing your back and bottom against your chair. Sink in to your body and relax.

3.   Now IMAGINE, PRETEND, SEE (whatever works for you) a connection from the base of your spine that goes through the floor and deep into the earth. As it goes down you feel the tug of gravity on your body, pulling you into your body.

4.   Once your grounding is in place tell yourself that everything that is not yours – fear, anxiety, anger, energy, or general discomfort you can't define – is going to release through the grounding connection, like water flushed down the toilet it is whisked away easily.

5.   Now bring your attention to the top of your head and imagine a golden ball of light, like a sun, hovering above you. Tell yourself you are now calling in all of your OWN energy into this light. You are calling it back from the people and places you fix or take care of. Call it back from the past and from the future. Your OWN energy is your awareness and consciousness, it is your wisdom,

power and clarity. Let this "sun" fill up with YOU, your unique vibration, and expand. Watch and feel it move down from above your head through your entire body, creating a bubble of your own energy all around you and down below your feet into the grounding connection.

6.   Envision a beautiful rose in front of you at the edge of this bubble, your aura. This is your protection rose that filters others' energy from entering your space. It is the energetic first impression others sense from you and establishes your physical boundary as well.

7.   Sit and bask in the light and energy of you. Breathe deeply. Notice how amazing it feels to feel just you. When you are ready, bend over and touch the floor. Stand up and reach for the sky. You are the bridge between heaven and earth.

Ba - Gua

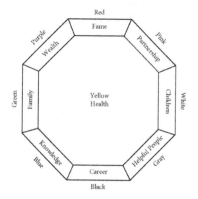

Notes

Chapter 3

1. Elaine N. Aron, The Highly Sensitive Person: How to Thrive When the World O[?]whelms You, (Broadway Books; Reprint edition, Jun[?] [?], 19[?])

2. Marti Olsen Lan[?] [?] Advantage: How Quiet People Can [?] in [?] World, (Workman Publishing [?] [?], [?]ary 1, 2002).

Chapter 4

1. Thomas Moore, [?] A Guide to Finding Your Way Throug[?] [?] New York, Penguin Group, 2004).

Chapter 8

1. Carol S. Dweck, Mindset: The New Psychology of Success, (Ballantine Books, Reprint, Updated edition, December 26, 2007).

Chapter 10

1.   Derek Rydell, *Shadow Dancing Meditation*, Adapted from the work of Derek Rydall. https://derekrydall.com/resources/
2.   Francis Weller, The Wild Edge of Sorrow: Rituals of Renewal and the Sacred Work of Grief, (North Atlantic Books, September 15, 2015).

Chapter 11

1.   Francis Weller, The Wild Edge of Sorrow: Rituals of Renewal and the Sacred Work of Grief, (North Atlantic Books, September 15, 2015).

Chapter 12

1.   Thomas Moore, Care of the Soul: How to Add Depth and Meaning to Your Everyday Life, (Harper, 1st edition, 1998).
2.   Thomas Moore, Care of the Soul, Twenty-fifth Anniversary Ed: A Guide for Cultivating Depth and Sacredness in Everyday Life, (Harper Perennial; Anniversary edition, January 26, 2016).
3.   Dr. Mark Hyman, The Blood Sugar Solution 10-Day Detox Diet: Activate Your Body's Natural Ability to Burn fat and Lose Up to 10lbs in 10 Days, (Yellow Kite, August 25, 2016).
4.   Paulo Coehlo, The Alchemist, (HarperOne Anniversary edition, April 15, 2014)

Chapter 13

1. Star Wars Episode IV: A New Hope. Twentieth Century Fox, 1977.

2. Brene Brown, The Gifts of Imperfection: Let Go of Who You Think You're Supposed to Be and Embrace Who You Are, (Hazelden Publishing; 1 edition, August 27, 2010).

Chapter 14

1. Wallace J Nichols, *Blue Mind: The Surprising Science That Shows How being Near, In, On or Under Water Can Make You Happier, Healthier, More Connected, and Better at What You Do*, (New York, Little Brown and Company, 2014)

2. *The Grounded*, Documentary by Steve Kroschel 2013

3. See www.mygroundedmovie.com/prescription-is-earth

Chapter 15

1. Rick Hanson, Hardwiring Happiness: The New Brain Science of Contentment, Calm, and Confidence, (Harmony, Sold by Random House LLC, October 8, 2013).

2. Shawn Achor, The Happiness Advantage – How a Positive Brain Fuels Success in Work and Life. New York, Currency, 2010.

3. Danielle LaPorte, The Desire Map Planner. www.Desiremap.com

4.   Eckhart Tolle, A New Earth: Awakening to Your Life's Purpose. New York, Penguin Group, 2006.

Chapter 18

1.   Kahlil Gibran, The Prophet, (originally published in 1923, Knopf; Pocket ed edition, February 21, 1995) – Paraphrase of original quote "The deeper that sorrow carves into your being, the more joy you can contain".

2.   Derek Rydall, Emergence: Seven Steps for Radical Life Change, (Atria Books/Beyond Words; Original ed. Edition, January 6, 2015).

Resources

1. Aron, Elaine N. The Highly Sensitive Person-How to Survive when the World Overwhelms You. New York, Broadway Books 1997.
2. Brown, Brené. The Gifts of Imperfection. Minnesota, Hazelden Books, 2010.
3. Coehlo, Paulo. The Alchemist. San Francisco, Harper San Francisco, 1993.
4. Dweck, Carol S. Mindset-The New Psychology of Success. New York, Ballantine Books, 2008.
5. Gibran, Kahlil. The Prophet. New York, Alfred Knopf Publishing, 1923.
6. Hanson, Rick. Hardwiring Happiness: The New Brain Science of Contentment, Calm, and Confidence. New York, Harmony Books, 2013.
7. Hillman, James. The Soul's Code: In Search of Character and Calling. New York, Random House, 1996.
8. Hyman, Mark. The Blood Sugar Solution 10-Day Detox Diet. New York, Little, Brown and Company, 2014.
9. Jenkinson, Stephen. Die Wise-A Manifesto for Sanity and Soul. Berkeley, CA, North Atlantic Books, 2013.

10. Junger, Sebastian. Tribe: On Homecoming and Belonging. New York, Grand Central Publishing, 2016.
11. Laney, Marti Olson. The Introvert Advantage-How to Thrive in an Extrovert World. New York, Workman Publishing, 2002.
12. LaPorte, Danielle. The Desire Map Planner. www.Desiremap.com
13. Moore, Thomas. Care of the Soul: A Guide for Cultivating Depth and Sacredness in Everyday Life. New York, HarperCollins Publishers, 1992.
14. Moore, Thomas. Dark Nights of the Soul: A Guide to Finding Your Way Through Life's Ordeals. New York, Penguin Group, 2004.
15. Nichols, Wallace J. Blue Mind: The Surprising Science That Shows How being Near, In, On or Under Water Can Make You Happier, Healthier, More Connected, and Better at What You Do. New York, Little Brown and Company, 2014.
16. Rydall, Derek. Emergence-Seven Steps for Radical Life Change. New York, Atria Paperback, 2015.
17. Tolle, Eckhart. A New Earth: Awakening to Your Life's Purpose. New York, Penguin Group, 2006.
18. Weller, Francis. The Wild Edge of Sorrow: Rituals of Renewal and the Sacred Work of Grief. Berkeley, CA, North Atlantic Books, 2015.
19. Whyte, David. River Flow: New and Selected Poems. Langley, WA, Many Rivers Press, 2007.

LET'S TALK!!

You're ready to find your light in the dark and live a richer life tied to your Soul! What's your next step? As thanks to you, I'm offering a special discounted mini-reading to jumpstart the journey back to your Self.

Sign up at https://julianovak.net/down-and-back/ to get your discount and stay in touch for future offers and events. I want to hear how you're doing too!!

Or email me at julia@julianovak.net and mention DOWN AND BACK to schedule a one-hour call.

For more information about Private Readings, my Awakening Intuition series, and Intuitive feng shui see www.julianovak.net

CPSIA information can be obtained
at www.ICGtesting.com
Printed in the USA
FSHW022248030319
55991FS

9 781732 319103